THE NATURE OF MORAL THINKING

Most recent texts in moral philosophy have either concentrated on practical moral issues or, if theoretical, have tended toward one-sided presentations of recent, fashionable views. Discussions of applied ethics are certain to be circumscribed unless underlying philosophical assumptions about deeper, more general issues are treated. Similarly, recent approaches to ethics are difficult to understand without a knowledge of the context of the historical views against which these approaches are reacting.

The Nature of Moral Thinking will satisfy the intellectually curious student, providing a solid and fair discussion of the classical philosophical questions about our moral thinking, surveying the main types of meta-ethical and normative ethical theories, while not excluding the more recent discussions of moral realism, of anti-realism, and of virtue morality. Francis Snare demonstrates that a very common kind of glib intellectualistic thinking about morality, especially in regard to relativism and subjectivism, is seriously flawed. Serious attention is given to the question of whether particular theories of the origins of morality (for example, Nietzsche's and Marx's) undermine morality.

All students and teachers of ethics and philosophy will find this book a solid survey of the foundations of ethics with emphasis on the question of the subjectivity or relativity of morality.

Francis Eugene Snare

Francis Snare, Senior Lecturer in the Department of Traditional and Modern Philosophy, Sydney University, died on 23 August 1990, after a struggle with cancer.

He was born on 4 June 1943, his home town being Tiffin, Ohio. After gaining a Bachelor of Arts degree from Kalamazoo College, Michigan, he went on to graduate studies at the University of Michigan at Ann Arbor, obtaining his doctorate in 1969. His supervisor was William Frankena. His first teaching position was as Assistant Professor of Philosophy at the University of Iowa, 1969–74. There followed a Research Fellowship at the Australian National University, 1974–9, broken by a one-semester appointment as Visiting Associate Professor at the University of Indiana. On the expiry of his Fellowship he was for a short time a Senior Tutor at Monash and then went to a lectureship at Sydney University in 1980.

For Francis, the classics of moral philosophy, together with political philosophy and the philosophy of law, were the centre of his philosophical concern, though he was well able to discuss and comment upon other issues. His work came to a focus in a searching criticism of Hume's moral philosophy. A book, *Morals, Motivation and Convention: Hume's Influential Doctrines*, was published in 1991 by Cambridge University Press. It was the great concern of his last months.

A very private person, he was an admirable and entirely principled colleague. As one came to know him, with his interesting conversation and at times sardonic but never bitter sense of humour, one came to like him more and more. He liked Australia, and became an Australian citizen. He bore his final illness courageously and uncomplainingly.

David Armstrong

THE NATURE OF
MORAL THINKING

Francis Snare

London and New York

First published 1992
by Routledge
11 New Fetter Lane, London EC4P 4EE

Simultaneously published in the USA and Canada
by Routledge
a division of Routledge, Chapman and Hall Inc.
29 West 35th Street, New York, NY 10001

Typeset in 10 on 12 point Garamond by
Intype, London
Printed in Great Britain by
TJ Press (Padstow) Ltd, Padstow, Cornwall

British Library Cataloguing in Publication Data
Snare, Francis
The nature of moral thinking.
I. Title
170

Library of Congress Cataloging in Publication Data
Snare, Francis.
The nature of moral thinking/Francis Snare.
p. cm.
Includes bibliographical references.
1. Ethics. 2. Ethical relativism. 3. Subjectivity. I. Title.
BJ1012.S545 1992
170—dc20 91–30981

ISBN 0–415–04708–0
ISBN 0–415–04709–9 (pbk)

Contents

Note

This book grew out of Francis Snare's first-year lectures in ethics at Sydney University. When he died, Francis was making final revisions to the manuscript. The revisions were completed by Michael McDermott, who has acted as editor. He had assistance from Stephen Gaukroger and Tony Lynch. Chapter 7 is, as Francis had planned from the start, based upon first-year lectures given by me on Plato's critique of Protagoras' relativistic theory of truth. Francis made several improvements on my treatment. Secretarial assistance was provided by Anthea Bankoff and Helen Brown.

Francis was a good man, a good colleague, and a good philosopher. We dedicate this book to his memory.

David Armstrong
University of Sydney
March 1991

1

Moral thinking and philosophical questions

EVERYDAY MORAL JUDGEMENTS

Philosophy does not arise out of mere idle speculation or other-worldly fantasizing. That is a caricature. It begins, at least, with what we do, say, and think in everyday life. On reflection, it can be seen that our everyday actions and thoughts already presuppose certain philosophical views, or else give rise to certain philosophical problems. To say 'I'm going to be practical, and not worry about philosophy' is simply to accept these conventional presuppositions uncritically and to pretend the problems do not arise. One does not really escape having (implicit) philosophical views, although most people avoid being critical or reflective about them.

More particularly, moral philosophy (or 'ethical theory', or 'ethics') typically begins with what is a rather deep-rooted part of everyday practice, i.e. the making of moral judgements and the thinking of moral thoughts. Some of the judgements are easily recognizable as moral because they involve the use of rather vener-able and even somewhat old-fashioned terms, such as 'moral', 'immoral', 'right', 'wrong', 'good', 'evil', 'bad', 'ought', 'obli-gation', 'duty', 'guilty', 'blameworthy', 'praiseworthy', 'noble', 'disgraceful', 'righteous', and 'virtuous'. However, other terms employed in moral judgements do not advertise themselves quite so obviously, e.g. 'is responsible for. . . ', 'is liable for. . . ', 'fair', 'unfair', 'owns' or 'has', 'mine', 'is part of one's job as. . . ', 'deserves', 'one's rights', 'human rights', 'is a thief', 'is a respon-sible person', 'was negligent', 'is a coward', and 'exploits the workers'. We say things like 'You just don't do A' (e.g. dob in your mates), which usually is a way of just saying 'A is wrong' or 'A ought not to be done', without of course actually using

1

such explicit language. Even to say 'A is permissible' seems to be a moral judgement, for it means that A is *not wrong*. (This is the *weak* sense of 'is permissible', as we shall see in a moment.) That is, it is the *denial* that a person has an obligation to *not* do A. But one would think that the denial of a moral judgement would itself be a moral judgement – it's just the other side of the particular moral issue. So even to say 'A is permissible' is to take a moral stand. When said seriously it is to think a moral thought.

Actually, many people intend 'A is permissible' in a *stronger* sense than this, one which entails, not only that doing A is not wrong (i.e. just 'is permissible' in the weak sense), but, further, that other parties (including law and society) *ought* not to interfere (at least in certain ways) with an individual's doing A. Such a judgement places as heavy an obligation on humankind as any Victorian moralist ever did, although it does it in a somewhat backhanded way. Thus 'permissivists', whatever they may pretend, do take a moral stand – and one which is, at first glance, no easier to defend than any other. It is a very common rhetorical ploy, these days, to put forward a distinct moral stance under the guise of *not* making moral judgements. The liberal and permissive values of our particular culture often make us feel guilty about making overt moral judgements. That seems so 'intrusive' and 'judgemental'. So we, unlike other cultures, go to great lengths to make our moral judgements seem like something else.

I invite anyone to go through a normal day without making or thinking a moral judgement. I do mean a normal day, not a day when one is unconscious or anaesthetized. Nor would one pass the test simply by taping one's mouth shut for a day. The question is whether one can avoid thinking moral thoughts in a normal social day. Sometimes people think they don't moralize because they don't use overt terms such as 'wrong' or 'ought'. They will say, for example, that Johnny's behaviour is 'antisocial' rather than 'naughty'. This might indeed mark some change in values. But more commonly the former term comes to do much the same work as the latter *in practice*, without any real change in values. Is it perhaps only a different sound?

SOME PROBLEMS WHICH ARISE

There are four important problems which arise concerning every-day moral judgements. The ancient Greeks were aware of most of these (which may partly explain why they pioneered work in moral philosophy). Problems arise from:

P1 Conflicts within one's moral code. For example, Sophocles' Antigone, or Sartre's example of the young Frenchman torn between the duty to join the resistance and his duty to support his ageing mother.

P2 Application of one's moral code to new circumstances. For example, the question of whether a foetus (at various stages) has any human rights, or the question of whether future generations have any claims on the earth's present resources.

Of course in everyday life we often make particular moral judgements (about particular occasions) without worrying about whether there are any general principles, or more general formulations, behind the particular judgements we make. It is usually only when we run into 'hard cases' that such worries arise. P1 and P2 are two important kinds of 'hard cases'. Thus problems like P1 and P2 provoke us into asking:

Q1 Are there any *general* principles of morality behind the various particular moral judgements we make? Or, what are the principles of morality?

But while a more complete *formulation* of our moral principles might do much to overcome problems such as P1 and P2, there are two further problems which arise in any case:

P3 Conflicts between moral codes of different societies. Herodotus in his *History* discussed such differences between societies, as do modern anthropologists, sociologists, and historians.

P4 The conflict between duty and self-interest: is it 'reasonable' to follow moral duty when it conflicts with self-interest? Some of the Greek sophists held that moral duty is mere 'convention' and that it is reasonable to 'follow nature' (for them, self-interest). Glaucon and Adeimantus in Book II of Plato's *Republic* set up the problem of conflict rather articulately.

P3 and P4 require more than a *formulation* of one's moral principles, they call for a *justification*. Such problems quite naturally provoke us to ask:

Q2 How can one justify (or ground, or prove) a moral judgement? And if we justify particular judgements by reference to some general formulation of a morality, how then do we justify that general formulation?

But how can we know what it is to justify a moral claim (either a particular judgement or a general formulation) until we first know what it is one is doing, or saying, in making a moral claim? We won't know how to justify (or refute, for that matter) what one is saying until we know first what it is he is saying or claiming. Thus, asking Q2 may well provoke one further to ask:

Q3 What, after all, *is* a moral judgement? Or, what exactly is one doing (or saying, or claiming, or meaning) in making a moral judgement? More particularly, what is meant by 'ought', or 'wrong', or 'good', or 'right'?

For some it may still not be too late to avoid these questions completely. One can slam this book shut, clap one's hands over one's ears and run screaming back to normal life, never to think about such things again. But if you have begun to worry even a little bit about questions like Q1, Q2, or Q3 it is probably too late. You have the disease. You are then asking philosophical questions. And merely to persist in everyday practice will not answer those questions. They require reflection and critical thinking.

METAPHYSICS, EPISTEMOLOGY, AND ETHICAL THEORY

So far we have considered how philosophical questions about morality can arise out of reflection on what we do and say in everyday life. However, there is another way in which such questions can arise. We can apply our general thoughts and theories in metaphysics (the theory of what ultimately exists) and epistemology (the theory of knowledge) to the special case of moral beliefs and judgements. Thus, if one is already doing philosophy, philosophical questions about morality in particular easily arise.

For example, in the course of thinking about epistemology one can come to wonder whether our apparent knowledge in regard to moral matters is like our knowing that a certain table is brown, or is more like knowing that seven is a prime number, or is more like knowing that bachelors are unmarried. Or does our moral knowledge perhaps belong to a special category of its own (perhaps with its own special 'faculty')? Or is there perhaps no such thing as 'knowledge' at all in matters of ethics? But one cannot really intelligently proceed with such issues without first taking up the basic issues in epistemology.

Again, in thinking about metaphysics one can come to wonder how the subject matter of moral judgements fits into one's philosophical account of what the world is made up of and the sorts of things which exist. In that regard the apparent ever-increasing success of the various sciences in describing and explaining what goes on in the world easily provokes the following philosophical question:

Q4 How does the subject matter of our ordinary moral judgements fit into the 'naturalistic' world, i.e. the world as described by the successful sciences? What is the place of moral 'values' in the world of scientific 'facts'? (This question will be raised again in chapter 5.)

Some people come to ask philosophical questions about moral judgements and thinking, not by beginning with ordinary moral judgements, but by already being interested in general philosophical questions about knowledge and reality. They then naturally wonder how whatever it is we are thinking in making moral judgements fits into their total philosophical view of what there is and what can be known.

NORMATIVE ETHICS AND META-ETHICS

Both Q1 and Q3 pose basic philosophical questions. However, many philosophers have thought they are importantly different. One influential strand in twentieth-century philosophical thought has considered the former question, Q1, to be a question in 'normative ethics' but the latter, Q3, to be a question of 'meta-ethics'. Perhaps we can illustrate what might be the difference between these two sorts of enquiry with respect to the special case of moral judgements of *right and wrong action*. (As we shall see, there are many kinds of moral judgements.)

Taking the special case of right action, Q1 asks what kinds of acts are right or what features of acts go with being right. As a first approximation, what philosophers call 'normative ethics' attempts to answer such questions. Ideally, normative ethics would provide us with some general formula, or formulas, for picking out the acts which are right. A possible schema for a normative ethics might be 'All acts with property F are right', where different philosophers might variously substitute for 'F' 'maximizing social happiness', 'avoiding suffering', or 'being commanded by God'. They have different ethical theories and disagree quite fundamentally. But they are all doing normative ethics. They are asking the same question ('What acts are right?'), even if they give different answers.

But this is only a first approximation. In fact any normative ethical theory attempts to do more than *identify* the right acts and is asking a bit more than Q1 asks. One could succeed in identifying right acts by means of features which have nothing to do directly with *why* they are right. (Compare the manual direction 'Next press the red button'. Here 'pushing the red button' identifies the right act, although the button's being red, rather than green, say, has nothing to do with *why* it is right.) Actually, a normative ethical theory claims that certain features or properties of acts are not only ones which right acts always happen to have, but are properties which *make* them right. The presence of those properties is the *reason why* those acts are right. They are 'right-making' properties. It is not a happy accident that all acts with property F happen to be right as well. Rather, property F tends to *make* an act right, it is a *reason* why an act is right, an act is right *because* it has F, or *in virtue of* its having F. It is of course a further interesting philosophical question just what we mean to be saying in speaking of 'reasons' and 'right-making' properties in this way. But what is clear is that normative ethics is concerned, not only to identify right acts, but also to say which of their properties it is which make them right.

By contrast, Q3 seems to be raising a somewhat different question. It does not, for example, ask which acts are in fact the right ones, or even what features make acts right. Instead it asks what is it to claim that an act is right. What is one saying of an act when one says it is right? Attempts to answer this sort of question are called 'meta-ethics' because the level of discourse seems to be one level prior to ('meta') the level of normative ethics. Now, the distinction between normative ethics ('What kinds of acts are right and what features of them make them right?') and meta-ethics ('What is it to say of an act that it is right, or that certain of its features make it right?') may seem very subtle indeed. Perhaps the following considerations will keep them apart:

False claims and disagreements

Normative ethics will presumably not be interested in those ethical claims which are 'false' (or unjustified, or ungrounded). But meta-ethics will be no less interested in 'false' claims than in 'true' ones. If someone makes a moral claim that is false, or at any rate one with which I disagree (e.g. 'marrying someone of another race is wrong'), it is no less appropriate (at the level of meta-ethics) to ask, 'But what is that person claiming (even if perhaps falsely) in claiming it is morally wrong?' Thus meta-ethics asks what it is that *anyone* means when he says something is wrong. Even if two people disagree whether an act is wrong, what exactly are they disagreeing about? What is it that the one disputant is thinking about the act which the other is denying?

Non-normative status

Normative ethics clearly takes a moral stand. It claims that certain acts are the right ones, and that certain properties make an act right. Thus normative ethics is 'evaluative' or 'normative'. By contrast it is not clear, at least, that meta-ethics is 'normative'. Many have thought it a purely factual, non-evaluative, philosophical enquiry. Meta-ethics does not, at first glance, take a normative stand on what particular acts are the right ones or even what makes acts right, but only investigates what it is people are claiming (or denying) who do take such stands. While normative ethics asks what acts are the right ones, meta-ethics asks only what it means to say (or deny) that an act is right (on whatever grounds).

Two kinds of 'is'

Philosophers distinguish between the 'is' of predication and the 'is' of identity. If I said 'This table is brown', I would be *predicating* 'brown' of this table and thus asserting that this table has the property of being brown. But of course no table is *identical* to the property of being brown. Brownness is, perhaps, something like the capacity to reflect a certain wavelength of electromagnetic radiation, or, perhaps, the capacity to cause a certain special sort of sensation or experience in us. But whatever it is exactly, it is not a certain table. Likewise, to ask (as in normative ethics) which acts are right is to ask which acts are we to predicate 'right' of, or which acts have rightness. But to ask (as in meta-ethics) what rightness itself *is* (is identical to) is quite another question. Whatever rightness may be, it is not identical to any act or even any class of acts. It is something acts have.

Admittedly, normative ethics tries to do more than just claim that certain acts are the right ones. Typically an ethical theory asserts that certain features of acts (e.g. preventing suffering, being commanded by God) are features that *make* them right (that an act is right *because* of certain features it has, that these features are the *reason why* it is right). But presumably the rightness of an act is not thought to be *identical to* the properties which make it right. Surely a normative ethical theory is not saying that an act is right *because* it has the feature of rightness. Rather, a normative ethics says that certain features (not identical to rightness) make an act have a further property as well, viz. rightness. By contrast, meta-ethics is not interested in taking some particular normative stand on what features make an act right. Instead, it is concerned with what it is to claim an act is right (on whatever grounds).

To be sure, some philosophers have thought that meta-ethics does have some important consequences for normative ethics. An adequate account of what rightness *is* (identity sense), or of what 'right' means, just might help show that certain substantive views on what acts *are* right (predicative sense) are either correct or mistaken. But we can leave open for now the question of just how normative ethics and meta-ethics might be related. The present task is simply to get some feel for why many philosophers have thought that doing meta-ethics is not quite the same thing as doing normative ethics.

'WHAT IS . . .?' QUESTIONS

We have seen how, beginning from everyday moral judgements and practice, moral philosophers end up asking fairly abstract 'What is . . .?' questions, e.g. 'What is rightness?', 'What is it to claim an act is right?' However, 'What is . . .?' questions are not peculiar to meta-ethics. They can be found in most areas of philosophy. Philosophers since Socrates have asked 'What is knowledge?', 'What is truth?', 'What are mental events?', 'What is causation?', 'What is time?', 'What are scientific laws?', and so on. Obviously philosophers are not interested in the everyday questions employing these concepts, e.g. questions like 'Does Jones *know* his wife is unfaithful?' or 'Does smoking *cause* cancer?' or 'Did Smith arrive *before* the murder?' Rather, philosophers are concerned with *meta*-questions such as 'What is it to allege (rightly, or even wrongly) that something (e.g. smoking) *causes* something else (e.g. cancer)?' Thus asking 'What is causation?' might be described as looking for the analysis of 'causation', or analysing 'causation'. Likewise asking 'What is rightness?' is frequently characterized as the project of looking for the correct analysis of 'rightness'. (Thus, not surprisingly, meta-ethics is sometimes called 'analytic ethics'.)

Socrates, notoriously, went around asking 'What is . . .?' questions. While the term 'analysis' is fairly recent, Socrates did speak of looking for the 'definition' of, say, knowledge, truth, virtue, justice. He considered the 'What is . . .?' question to be the peculiarly philosophical one.

A good example of Socrates' procedure is to be found in Plato's dialogue *Euthyphro*. Euthyphro, perhaps a rather self-righteous man, is on his way to make charges in court against his father. The father found it necessary to bind a labourer who had become drunk and committed a violent murder. However, the father subsequently forgot about or neglected the labourer bound and lying in a ditch, so that he died. So Euthyphro is off to prosecute his own father for this negligent homicide. Now Socrates is a little shocked at this, and in this he perhaps reflects the values of ancient Greek society rather than ours. The conventional Greek attitude was probably that the labourer was of a low class anyway, that he was a violent murderer, that the father didn't actively kill him but only neglected him, and, most importantly, that what Euthyphro owes to his father, family, and kin cannot in the least be offset by concern for some unrelated, lowborn criminal. Of course in our society it would be more common to take the side of Euthyphro and speak of the human and civil rights of the labourer. But Socrates is a little surprised at the unconventional stand Euthyphro is taking and wonders just how he can defend his position. In response, Euthyphro defends his act as a 'pious' (or 'holy', or 'righteous') one. Thus the dialogue begins with a particular normative claim made in everyday life. However, Socrates, in typical fashion, immediately pushes Euthyphro back to the *meta*-level. If Euthyphro can justify such a claim, or even know what he is claiming, he must at the very least know what piety *is* (i.e. what it is to claim that an act is pious).

Euthyphro's first 'definition' (*Euth.* 5d) makes it clear he fails to appreciate the question. He gives *examples* of pious acts. 'For example,' he says, 'what I am now doing.' But Socrates' question does not call for a *list* (even an exhaustive list) of acts which *are* (predicative sense) pious. Socrates wants to know what it is that all pious acts have in common, what being pious *is* (identity sense), what is being said of an act when it is claimed (rightly, or wrongly) to be pious. Eventually Euthyphro produces a definition (*Euth.* 9d) which is at least of the right form: Being pious *is the same thing as* being pleasing to (being loved by) all the gods. The 'is' here is the 'is' of identity. Note that it is not enough that all pious acts happen also to be acts which (for one reason or another) are pleasing to the gods. Rather, Euthyphro's claim, if it is a definition, is that the property of being pious is nothing more or less than the property of being pleasing to the gods. While Socrates goes on to give an interesting argument against this particular definition, he has at least got Euthyphro to do philosophy. Euthyphro is proposing an analysis of what piety is and not merely giving a list of the acts, or sorts of acts, which are pious.

ADVANCED QUESTIONS TO THINK ABOUT (BUT NOT TO DECIDE RIGHT AWAY)

1 How is it that we seem to know such things as:

   (a) To assert that *A is permissible* is (at least) to assert that *A is not wrong*.
   (b) To assert that *A is permissible* is (at least) to assert that *it is not obligatory not to do A*?

Are claims like (a) and (b) themselves moral judgements, or are they some other sort of judgement about moral judgements? Are (a) and (b) true?

2 Is there something wrong with the following argument (where 'A' stands for some action)?

   (i) Either a proposition is true or else the proposition which is its denial is true.

Therefore, applying (i),

(ii) Either 'A is wrong' is true or else 'It is not the case that A is wrong' is true.

(iii) Both 'A is wrong' and 'It is not the case that A is wrong' are moral propositions.

Therefore, from (ii) and (iii),

(iv) Some moral proposition *is true* (even if we may not *know* which it is).

3 If the negation of a moral judgement is also a moral judgement, what would it be like to make no moral judgements at all? What would it be like to make no value judgements?

4 In Dostoevsky's *Brothers Karamazov* is found the claim 'If God is dead, then everything is permissible'. Is the assertion *'Everything* is permissible' a moral judgement? Does the *Karamazov* claim really entail that even if God is dead there will still be this true moral proposition?

5 Imagine what it would be like for everything to be permissible. For example, sitting on a park bench isn't wrong. But neither is it wrong for others to threaten one, or push one off, or burn the bench. Nor is passing moral judgements on bench-sitting wrong, and so on.

6 What is the difference between *asserting* that it is *not* the case that A is wrong and *not asserting* that A is wrong? Instead of asserting 'Everything is permissible', might one avoid all moral judgements simply by not asserting (or thinking!) any moral judgement (even the thought that something is permissible)?

7 Is there a difference between

(a) A is not wrong (or right, or permissible).

and:

(b) It is not the case that A is wrong (or right, or permissible).

such that (a), but not (b), makes a moral judgement, and so that asserting (b) does not commit one to (a)?

8 Is it really true that one cannot know, or be justified in making, everyday claims such as 'A is pious' (or 'Smoking causes cancer' or 'Jones arrived before the murder') unless one is ready to defend an explicit philosophical account of what piety is (or

what causation is, or what time is)? (See Moore (1959) for a classic discussion.) Why couldn't Euthyphro just say his view was the normative one that being pleasing to the gods *makes* acts pious but not the meta-ethical one that the latter property just *is* the former?

FURTHER READING

Straightforward introductory discussions at the level of this chapter can be found in Brandt (1959: ch. 1) and Frankena (1973: ch. 1). More generally, a very readable introductory text remains Hospers (1961). Recent texts surveying theories in normative ethics and/or meta-ethics include Finnis (1983), Rachels (1986), and Mackie (1977). Recent works which are not surveys so much as justifications for particular views will be mentioned, as relevant, in later chapters. So also will those texts which strongly emphasize certain recent developments.

While philosophers today are perhaps more inclined to question this distinction, the classic discussion of how normative ethics and meta-ethics are distinct is Moore (1903). Moore's discussion is advanced and extremely subtle.

A useful encyclopaedia of philosophy is Edwards (1967), and a similarly useful dictionary is Flew (1983). These give references to the standard philosophical positions and the meanings of specialized philosophical terms.

But probably the best way to dig into the philosophical issues raised in this chapter is just to go to the beginnings and read Plato's *Euthyphro* for oneself. Not only is the dialogue engaging, but one is getting philosophy first hand. For a more advanced discussion of Socratic definition see Robinson (1971). Also a useful account of Socrates' philosophy can be found in Guthrie (1962).

2

Authoritarian ethics and subjectivist ethics

THEISM AND MORALITY

Because of the past influence of religion in our culture, many people (even some atheists) find it plausible to suppose that moral philosophy will have to be based on religious or theistic propositions. (It is worth noticing, though, that the ancient Greek philosophers never saw much need to base moral philosophy on religious beliefs, and most modern moral philosophers have not done so.)

How could morality be 'based on' religion? Not every way in which religious or theistic propositions might be *relevant to* moral thinking amounts to *basing* moral philosophy on such propositions. In particular, the following three claims, even if true, would not show that moral philosophy has to be based on religion. Consider, first:

(1) God's threats of punishment (or perhaps one's belief in them) provide a strong (even if somewhat crass) *motive* for being moral.

We sometimes refer to a motive for doing something as a 'reason' for doing it, but this is not to be confused with a *justifying reason*. The threat of a fine, for example, does much to motivate people not to park in certain areas, but the fine is not the reason that parking there is wrong, it's not what *makes* it wrong. Likewise, God's threats may merely *motivate* people to do what is already right, for justifying reasons having nothing to do with the threat. (For a different view, see Williams (1972).)

Here is a second way in which religious propositions can be relevant:

13

(2) Fact-claiming theistic propositions can figure as minor premisses in moral arguments which have non-theistic propositions as ultimate moral premisses.

Here is an example of (2):

(a) Each individual ought to maximise total social happiness.
(b) What God commands individuals will in fact always maximize total social happiness (perhaps because God desires human happiness).

Therefore

(c) Each individual ought to do what God commands.

Notice that while the theistic premiss (b) is a part of a moral argument for the moral conclusion (c), (b) is not itself a moral judgement. Furthermore, the ultimate moral premiss of the argument, (a), is put forward with no obvious religious or theistic basis. Thus theistic propositions may occur in moral arguments without the ultimate moral premisses being based on theistic propositions. Notice also that the person who accepts this argument does not think we ought to obey God's commands just because they are his commands, but because doing so is a means of maximizing social happiness.

Third, references to God might appear in the content of moral judgements, even if morality is not based on God. Thus, we might consider the (moral) claim:

(3) We have some duties owed *to* God (if he exists).

Of course (3) is compatible with our having many other duties owed to others besides God, e.g. to our children, our parents, our promisees, our creditors, the needy, legitimate authority. Perhaps we ought to obey God just as we ought (in decent regimes) to obey the police and court orders. But while God (like our children etc.) may be the *beneficiary* or *object* of a moral obligation, it no more follows that morality is *based on* God than it follows that morality is based on our children, our promisees, or the courts.

Now the claims in (1) through (3), and others like them, are important claims and are what many religious persons want to assert and defend. However, none of these claims involves bringing theistic or religious propositions into the most fundamental

14

levels of normative ethics or into meta-ethics. What, then, would it be like to bring God or religion into normative ethics and meta-ethics? Here are two examples (as applied to moral judgements of *rightness*):

(4) (A theistic meta-ethical theory:) Being right just *is* being commanded by God.

The above is not to be confused with:

(5) (A theistic normative ethical theory:) The one and only feature which *makes* an act right is God's having commanded it (i.e. acts are right *because* God commands them).

I take it that in thinking that a certain feature of an act (e.g. God's commanding it) 'makes' it right, or is the 'reason' why it is right, one is supposing that this feature, or reason, is something other than the rightness itself. It is a feature which requires that something else, rightness, be present. Thus, to maintain the normative ethical theory in (5) involves abandoning the meta-ethical analysis in (4), and vice versa. Theists must make up their minds just how they are going to try to bring God into their moral philosophy.

Finally, neither the meta-ethical claim in (4) nor the normative ethical claim in (5) should be confused with another claim: God's commands are merely good indicators (perhaps absolutely reliable guides) to what is morally right, although they are not any part of what being right is or what makes something right. (An analogy: Consider how the *Handbook of Chemistry and Physics* is a quite reliable guide to various physical data and constants, but no part of the reason for their being so.) Thus we must also consider:

(6) While any act A is right *if and only if* God commands A, neither (4) nor (5) is the case.

To accept (6) is to think of God as an 'authority' in much the same way that the *Handbook of Chemistry and Physics* is a scientific authority. While (6) is an important thesis, and perhaps all that many religious persons want to assert, it does not really base moral philosophy on God or theistic propositions.

In short, to hold either (4) or (5), unlike holding any of (1), (2), (3), or (6), is to think that moral philosophy is based in some interesting way on theistic propositions. But any such attempt to found moral philosophy on theistic propositions has two fairly high hurdles to clear:

(A) G.E. Moore's influential 'open question' argument, which
     claims to show that (4) commits the 'naturalistic fallacy'.
This argument will be discussed in chapters 5 and 6.

(B) Socrates' famous argument in *Euthyphro*, 9e–11b.
We take up Socrates' argument in the rest of this chapter.

As we saw in chapter 1, Socrates' argument is directed toward
a definition of the moral term 'piety' as being synonymous with
'being pleasing to the gods', rather than to a definition of 'rightness' as being synonymous with 'being commanded by God'.
However, his argument is easily altered to apply to the latter as
well.

Actually there seem to be *two* arguments implicit in Socrates'
discussion (although he does not clearly distinguish them). One
attacks (4), theistic meta-ethics, while the other attacks (5), theistic
normative ethical theory.

Theistic meta-ethics

We take up the dialogue where we left it in chapter 1 (*Euth.* 9d).
Euthyphro has said that an act's being pious just *is* (identity) its
being loved by all the gods. Socrates likes to call this a 'definition'.
While there is some controversy about just what Socrates meant
by 'definition', let us suppose that Euthyphro was putting forth
a meaning claim about words. (In chapter 6 we will see that some
meta-ethical theories are doing something quite different from
this.) He is claiming that a certain phrase means the same thing
as ('$=_{df}$') another phrase:

(i) 'Being pious' $=_{df}$ 'being loved by all the gods' (9e).

But the claim in (i) is only one of the things Euthyphro wants to
hold about the gods. He has a further important belief as well.
Socrates brings this out in (10d) when he asks Euthyphro *why*
the gods love all the things which happen to be pious. Euthyphro,
priding himself on his high-mindedness, wants to think that the
gods have noble rather than base motives. So he wants to insist
that the gods love those acts just because they are pious ones, and
not simply for other reasons. For example, it's not merely that
they delight in seeing humans scamper about to satisfy their arbitrary whims. Nor is it that they need certain services from humans,

for that would make the gods dependent on us for certain things. Thus Euthyphro is concerned also to hold:

(ii) The reason the gods love the acts which are pious is that these acts are pious (i.e. the gods love such acts on account of the piety of these acts).

Now what Socrates wants to show is that there is something inconsistent about trying both to hold the meta-ethical theory in (i) and to attribute to the gods the motivation in (ii). Socrates' argument here has the form of a *reductio ad absurdum*. It proceeds by *supposing* that (i) and (ii) are true and then showing that something absurd would follow from this. It goes like this. If the meaning claim in (i) really were correct, it would follow that in (ii) we could substitute 'being loved by all the gods' for 'pious', and the sentence resulting from this change would have to be saying something just as true as the original, (ii). Thus, holding (i) and (ii) together would require that one also hold

(iii) The reason the gods love the acts which are pious is that they are acts loved by all the gods.

But, Socrates says in (10e), the fact that one loves something cannot itself be one's reason for loving it. Thus (iii) is the absurdity which Socrates thinks follows from trying to hold (i) and (ii) simultaneously. And there is good reason for thinking that (iii) is an absurdity, provided we take it in the way it has to be taken if it is to follow from (i) and (ii). It is true that when asked why I like something, I might reply in an irritated tone of voice, 'Because I like it.' But this seems to be a way of saying that I don't have any reasons for liking it, I just do. Certainly not all of our wants have reasons behind them. For example, some are just brute desires. But in (ii) and (iii) Euthyphro is speaking of cases where things really are loved for some further reason (and are not just the object of a brute yen). Socrates thinks it absurd that one's further reason for loving something could be precisely one's loving it.

Now if premises (i) and (ii) require that (iii) be true as well, and if (iii) is false because an absurdity, this still does not show that (i) in particular must be false. All that this *reductio* argument shows is that *not both* of premises (i) and (ii) can be true. The conclusion of Socrates' argument here is not that a specific proposition is false. Rather it has the form of a dilemma. Euthyphro cannot, as he wanted, hold both (i) and (ii). He must give up one of the two. And while it may be very difficult for Euthyphro to decide, it is still up to Euthyphro which to give up.

That it is a dilemma that follows from Socrates' argument is important in a slightly different example. Consider the theist who wants to hold both

(i') 'Being right' $=_{df}$ 'being commanded by God'

and

(ii') God commands those acts which are right just *because* they are right.

Socrates will argue here, analogously to his argument with Euthyphro, that because an absurdity follows from supposing both of these (viz. that God's reason for commanding is just that he commands), one of them must be abandoned. The theist is presented with a dilemma. In the history of philosophy and theology some theists, recognizing the force of Socrates' argument, have adhered to (i) but abandoned (ii). Their deepest concern is to continue to hold that being right just *is* being commanded by God. But in that case God's alleged moral goodness seems to come to little more than his not acting contrary to his own will. It will not be a matter of his having more high-minded motivations, such as his commanding acts because he already sees they are right. The gain is a solidly theistic meta-ethics, but the loss is any substantive notion of God's moral goodness. The theists who have chosen this side of the dilemma may be called 'voluntarists'. Rightness is, for the voluntarist, just a matter of God's will.

The alternative, 'anti-voluntarism', saves the substance of God's moral goodness, but at a cost. This view holds that God commands acts because he sees that they are right, quite independently of his willing them. This might even make God's commands an utterly reliable indication of moral rightness in the way theistic proposition (6) above asserts. But, even so, being right is something other than being commanded by God. What it is is presumably the topic of meta-ethics. At this point, the anti-voluntarist thinks, even God must stop commanding and begin doing meta-ethics.

Theistic normative ethics

I also find a slightly different argument in the *Euthyphro*. In 10a–c Socrates asks whether

(i) Acts are pious *because* the gods like them.

or

(ii) The gods like those acts which are pious *because* they are pious.

Likewise we might ask whether

(i′) Acts are right *because* God commands them.

or

(ii′) God commands those acts which are right *because* they are right.

Socrates thinks, in each case, that one cannot hold both. But what is his argument? Because no meaning claim is involved, in the first member of either of these pairs, we cannot use any such thing to make a substitution as we did in the preceding section. Even so, Socrates seems to think these are mutually exclusive alternatives between which Euthyphro must choose. Unfortunately, the actual argument Socrates gives is seriously flawed. (One must not suppose Socrates always has the better argument.) He argues that you cannot maintain pairs like the above because you cannot sensibly maintain both 'x because y' and 'y because x' at the same time (see his examples about carrying and being carried at *Euth*. 10b–c). This argument fails to apply to the above pairs because it assumes that the 'because' in the first claim is the same as the 'because' in the second. But this is not so in (i′) and (ii′), for example. The 'because' in the latter gives God's reason (i.e. his *motive*) for commanding. However, the 'because' in the former is not anyone's reason (i.e. *motive*) for doing anything. Rather, it gives the reason (i.e. *justification*) why an act is right. (Thus Socrates' analogies to carrying and seeing are quite misleading.)

Yet I agree with Socrates that (i′) and (ii′) seem to be mutually exclusive, but for a different reason. To assert both does seem to lead to some kind of absurdity. Consider the question 'Is such and such an act right?' Now if (i′) is the truth in normative ethics, (i′) is precisely what God uses to answer this question (for he believes things for the right reasons). But this only tells him the act in question would be right *if* he commanded it, and that on no other basis could it be right. But this hypothetical proposition does not tell God whether it *is* right. Now at that point he might give short shrift to the issue simply by commanding the action (on a whim, or to settle the matter), thus making it right as per (i') – *except* that, according to (ii'), God is not motivated in that sort of way. Whims, exasperation, or whatever are never sufficient motivation for God when it comes to commanding right acts. So, God sees, the issue really comes down to 'Shall I command this act *on account of its rightness*?' But God's answer here will be 'Yes' *only if* he already (i.e. independently, in the order of his reasoning) believes the act is right. So, for God, the issue comes back to 'Is this act right?' But that is precisely the question with which he began. (i') and (ii') together trap God in a logical circle. His decision to command depends on his prior belief in the rightness of the act commanded, but a rational belief about rightness depends precisely on what God decides to command. The fault here, of course, is not in God but in a normative ethics, (i'), which in the presence of a morally motivated God, (ii'), becomes quite vacuous, a pseudo-ethics.

Given that this logical circle is unacceptable, the theist is, as before, provided with a dilemma. If he adopts (i') as his normative ethical theory, he must reject (ii'), a substantive notion of a morally motivated God. God's commands, and morality, will depend on his whims or whatever. Alternatively, the theist can preserve some substantive notion of a morally good God but then concede that even God must do normative ethical theory (without considering his own commands) in order to discern what acts are right. Unless there is a flaw in Socrates' argument (something worth considering carefully), the theist is presented with a dilemma. There may be perfectly acceptable ways of choosing, given this dilemma. But what the theist cannot do is simply ignore Socrates.

GENERALIZING SOCRATES' ARGUMENT

Philosophers are not only interested in particular arguments (e.g. Socrates' particular argument against Euthyphro's two particular claims) but also in the *logical form* of those arguments. In that regard we might notice that nothing really rests on certain of the particular features of Euthyphro's two claims. For example, it would seem not particularly important that Euthyphro puts forward two propositions involving the notion 'is pious'. In fact we've examined a more contemporary pair of propositions involving the notion 'is morally right' instead, and exactly the same difficulty seemed to arise. Likewise nothing particularly seems to rest on the fact that Euthyphro's propositions make reference to *the gods' loving* certain acts. The modern parallel concerned, instead, *God's commanding* certain acts. As long as the substitution of 'is right' for 'is pious' and of 'commanded by God' for 'loved by all the gods' is carried out systematically throughout both of the two propositions, we do not seem to alter the logical form that gives rise to the Socratic dilemma. Because some details are not relevant to the generation of the dilemma, we may expect there will be a large number of 'Euthyphro dilemmas' beyond the two particular ones we discussed as examples. So it is worthwhile to ask just how far this result can be generalized. What form must a pair of propositions have to be a genuine Euthyphro-like pair generating a Euthyphro dilemma?

It does seem crucial to Socrates' objection that the 'because' in Euthyphro's proposition (ii) be the motivational 'because'. His objection takes up what is involved in this motivation. More specifically, proposition (ii) speaks of the motivating reasons the gods (or God) have for loving (or commanding) certain things. It is a claim about the reasons why the gods (God) love (command) as they do. But, typically, beings capable of having reasons can have reasons *for* a number of different things. Persons can have reasons for *doing* certain things (e.g. commanding); persons can have reasons for *feeling* in certain ways (e.g. loving); again, persons can even have reasons for *believing* certain things. For convenience let's use the expression 'person P has S toward act A' as a formula to cover any case where an agent A is in a particular psychological state (such as believing, desiring, feeling) toward A, or is engaged in a particular activity in regard to act A, where it makes sense to ask just what reasons P has for believing, desiring, feeling, acting (i.e. having S) in just that way toward A. It would seem that any pair with the following *form* will be subject to precisely the same sort of argument that Socrates raised against Euthyphro's particular pair of propositions. Any such pair will constitute a Euthyphro-like pair:

Schema 1

(i) Act A is morally right because God has S toward A.
(ii) The reason why God has S toward A is (or involves) his first believing A to be morally right.

Here we may substitute for 'has S toward' variously 'commands us to do', 'believes to be morally right', 'likes us to do', 'wills us to do', 'punishes us if we don't do', etc. Thus we can generate a great many Euthyphro dilemmas. What is important is only that the reason God has S toward A involves his already believing A to be morally right. The fact that Socrates' point against Euthyphro has force, not merely against the original pair, but equally against any pair whatsoever sharing the form of schema 1, means that Socrates' argument is rather more powerful than might first appear. It has more application than just against Euthyphro's particular views.

AUTHORITARIAN ETHICS

Many philosophers have thought the Socrates argument is even more powerful, capable of even more generalization, than suggested by schema 1. They have thought the real moral behind Socrates' argument against Euthyphro could be extended even beyond theistic ethics to apply to certain kinds of non-theistic ethical positions as well. They have thought the real point behind Socrates' objection could be made in regard to any kind of 'authoritarian' view in moral philosophy, not just theistic ones. They would say that there will be just as much of a threat of a Socratic dilemma with any view that uses something other than God as a source of moral rightness, e.g. society, one's culture, the church as an institution, certain texts, the voice of conscience, law, democratic institutions or parliamentary procedures, the majority, the general will, society's enforced punishments, socially held values, socially held beliefs, or even the views of some text in moral philosophy. In short, does anything in Socrates' objection really depend on it's being *God's* having S toward A? Wouldn't a similar dilemma arise in regard to the acts, beliefs, mental states of *any* agent or entity claimed to occupy the role of source of moral rightness and wrongness? We might see this better by considering pairs of propositions with this form:

Schema 2

(i) Action A is morally right because agent P has S toward A.
(ii) The reason why agent P has S toward A is (or involves) P's first believing A to be morally right.

However, this further generalization (to include agents and entities other than God) does make a bit of a difference to whether Socrates' objection continues to work in quite the same way. For now, strictly speaking, there is no absurdity in both (i) and (ii) being true, provided that the moral beliefs which, according to (ii), motivate P to have S toward A are *ill-formed* moral beliefs, i.e. ones not based on (i), the moral view we are trying to imagine true concurrently with (ii). That is, both (i) and (ii) can be true, provided the agent P forms his moral beliefs, not on the basis of (i), but on the basis of some other benighted moral view. Here is an example. Someone might consistently hold that

(i″)   Acts are morally right only because society generally approves of such acts in a certain way.

and also that

(ii″) The precise way that society approves of such acts is on account of their supposed moral rightness.

These could both be true, *provided* society's reason for thinking such acts right is *not* (i″), its own approval, but something else instead, i.e. some benighted superstitious moral view. The acts of which society approves would in fact become morally right, but not quite for the reasons society supposes. Only if a belief in (i″) became widespread throughout society would there be a Euthyphro dilemma.

Thus it would appear there is no real Euthyphro difficulty unless we add a further proposition to schema 2 to get the following incompatible triad (a *tri*-lemma, perhaps):

Schema 3

(i) Action A is morally right because agent P has S toward A.
(ii) The reason why agent P has S toward A is (or involves) P's first believing A to be morally right.
(iii) Agent P's belief that A is morally right is founded solely on the ground given by (i).

In the theistic cases (schema 1) it was unnecessary to add proposition (iii) explicitly. It goes without saying, for the theist, that God gets things right. Thus if (i) is the correct moral theory, then God knows it and forms his beliefs about moral rightness and wrongness on that basis. He not only believes what is true, but knows why it is true. If we wish, we may think of schema 3 applying to the theistic case, but where the theist will automatically think (iii) is true if he thinks (i) is true. So, for the theist, it will come down to a dilemma between holding (i) and holding (ii). However, in the non-theistic cases where a moral authority is claimed to be the source of right and wrong, proposition (iii) will not automatically follow from proposition (i). There will be a tri-lemma rather than a dilemma. Propositions (i) and (ii) could both be held, but only if one then conceded that the 'authority' forms its own moral beliefs on something other than the correct view. The moral 'authority' will form its moral beliefs on some superstitious grounds, not realizing that it is precisely its own mental state or action toward an act that makes it right or wrong. If some moral authority can, by acting or adopting a certain state of mind, make acts morally right, that authority cannot have a moral motivation for so acting or feeling, or, if it does, that moral motivation must involve failing to understand its own powers to make acts right.

There is an interesting point to be made about all authoritarian ethical theories. While such theories hold that rightness and wrongness are actual properties that acts have, they nevertheless deny that rightness and wrongness are *intrinsic* properties. Rightness is not a matter of anything about the act in itself, but is rather a matter of how an outside agent, P, acts or reacts toward that act.

Authority and authoritarian ethics

The generalized version of the Euthyphro difficulty in schema 3 raises a certain problem for any authoritarian ethics (including, of course, theistic authoritarian ethics). But it is important not to exaggerate this result. For one thing, the Socratic argument does not refute all ethical theories of form (i), but only argues that one cannot hold the corresponding (ii) and (iii) along with (i). But even where, because one does want to hold things like (ii) and (iii), Socrates' argument leads one to reject authoritarian moral

theories, one must not exaggerate even this result. Socrates' argument does raise difficulties for authoritarian ethical theories, but
this must not be exaggerated into a general *epistemological* difficulty about knowledge in moral matters. Socrates' argument has
nothing at all to do with that all-purpose argument stopper and
rhetorical escape device 'Who's to judge?', or even 'Who are *you*
to judge?' The point of such questions is sometimes to express a
certain epistemological scepticism about moral matters. It might
be to suggest that no one can have any rational grounds for
forming beliefs in moral matters, i.e. that there is no such thing
as moral knowledge. Or, if not that, it is at least to suggest
that no one can ever be better placed, more rational, or more
knowledgeable than anyone else in moral matters. We will in fact
examine some views in later chapters which hold that at some
ultimate level moral matters are not true or false and that, consequently, there can be nothing like knowledge in regard to such
things. But it is important to realize that nothing in Socrates'
Euthyphro argument tends in that direction. To have doubts about
'authoritarian ethics' in particular does not mean having general
doubts about knowledge in moral matters. To have the latter
doubts is a very much more radical matter. Not all ethical theories
(e.g. those in chapter 3) *can* be put into the form of (i) in schema
3. Not all ethical theories hold that rightness and wrongness are
not intrinsic properties of acts, but only a matter of how some
special agent (the authority) acts or reacts in regard to such acts.
Socrates' Euthyphro argument only applies to theories which do
hold just that.

In this connection we need to distinguish two senses of the
word 'authority'. The first is the *epistemic* sense. An authority in
this sense is someone who is better placed, more informed, more
rational, more capable of assessing the relevant evidence, perhaps
more to be trusted to convey information accurately, etc. than is
ordinary. We speak of scientific authorities in this sense. Whether
there also can be authorities in moral matters in this (epistemic)
sense is a matter of dispute. But it cannot be said that Socrates'
argument has given us any reason to think there are not. It isn't
even addressing that issue, i.e. the possibility of moral knowledge
and morally knowledgeable persons. Who shall judge? Well, perhaps, some edge is to be given the person better placed to know
the details, with a reputation for fairness, etc. Of course what that
person says, thinks, feels, etc. won't be what *makes* it right. But,

even so, he might be a bit more likely to come up with the correct conclusion than others. Some people, 'moral sceptics', think there cannot be moral authorities in the epistemic sense because there is no such thing as moral knowledge. But Socrates' argument does nothing to rule out the possibility of morally knowledgeable persons. That is simply another matter.

Another sense of 'authority' is the *empowerment* sense. We see this notion at work in many of our legal and moral conventions. With certain legal roles (legislator, judge, parent, policeman, property-owner) goes the power to alter or even create new rules and norms. The occupiers of such roles can alter the legal obligations of others in certain respects. For example, those who occupy the role of legislator can, by certain procedures, bring new laws into existence or repeal old ones. Likewise a property-owner can, by either giving or refusing permission, make a certain act of mine either permissible entry or trespass. 'Who shall say?' Well, perhaps those occupying the appropriate role (legislator, property-owner, parent, etc.). 'Who are you to judge?' might be a way of saying you are not empowered to make acts right or wrong in the matter at hand. You don't occupy the relevant role to do so.

Are there *ultimate* authorities in moral matters in the empowerment sense of 'authority'? If so, then some version of authoritarian ethics is true. Some agent P is such that something like his commands, statements, choices, beliefs, or feelings are ultimately what *make* acts right or wrong. He is an authority in the empowerment sense, not in the epistemic sense. He doesn't *discover* which acts are right, his actions or reactions *make* them right.

Socrates' Euthyphro argument is addressed to views (like Euthyphro's) that suppose there are ultimate moral authorities in the empowerment sense. It applies, as per schema 3, to any authoritarian ethics (including theistic ones). However, it does not address at all the question of whether there can be moral authorities in the epistemic sense. It leaves entirely open the question of whether there are moral authorities merely in the sense of morally knowledgeable persons.

SUBJECTIVIST NORMATIVE ETHICS

Philosophical arguments have a nasty habit of being generalizable and applying to cases not originally foreseen. Fashionable and sophisticated people are often quite happy to see theistic ethics and, more generally, authoritarian ethics become entangled in Socratic difficulties. What they may not notice is that the same difficulties entangle some of the fashionable views as well. In particular Socrates' objection is just as hard on certain 'subjectivist' ethical theories as it is on authoritarian ethical theories.

In a certain respect 'subjectivism' is a natural extension of 'authoritarianism'. Both share a common assumption. We can illustrate this in the form of an imaginary intellectual history. Suppose one began with a theistic ethic. One assumed that acts had to be *made* right by something like God's commands, thoughts, feelings, etc. Notice that doubts about God's existence might eventually lead one to give up theistic ethics *without* necessarily giving up the underlying assumption that acts can be right only by being made right by the action or reaction of some appropriate agent. One then might look for a substitute to occupy the role of God in theistic ethics. Some might continue to find this role-occupier in something outside themselves, e.g. in the actions and reactions of something like one's culture, the majority, or society. Such a view would be authoritarian without being theistic any more. But there is another possibility as well. One might put oneself into the role formerly occupied by God in theistic ethics. One might come to think that it is one's own actions or reactions, instead of God's actions or reactions, which literally make an act right ('for oneself', at least). While the term 'subjectivist' will be given some different employments in later chapters (where we discuss subjectivist *meta-ethics*), we can call the above view a 'subjectivist *normative* ethics'.

Subjectivism often passes itself off as the exact opposite of authoritarian ethics. Instead of some outside authority being empowered to make acts right, it is something inside that does this. Subjectivists claim to be 'inner-directed' rather than 'other-directed'. But in a certain important respect subjectivist ethics is very similar to authoritarian ethics. The subjectivist ethical theory can also be put in the form of the first proposition of schema 3:

(i) Action A is right (for me?) because I have S toward A.

Different versions of subjectivism will make different kinds of substitutes for 'have S toward', e.g. 'act in a certain way toward', 'have a certain belief toward', 'have certain motives or intentions in regard to', 'have certain feelings toward'.

Whether a Euthyphro difficulty can arise for the subjectivist will depend on the precise nature of the acting, believing, intending, or

27

feeling in question. Euthyphro difficulties would seem to arise for the subjectivist only if the subjectivist also supposes that

(ii) The reason why I, the subjectivist, have S toward A rests on my already believing A to be morally right.

and also

(iii) I form that belief precisely on the subjectivist grounds of (i).

One of the three claims must then go (although not necessarily the subjectivist theory of (i), of course).

CASES TO CONSIDER (BUT NOT NECESSARILY DECIDE RIGHT AWAY)

Do the following sets of propositions get into Euthyphro-like difficulties? Does it make a difference that God, and his usual characteristics, are not involved in these cases?

Set 1

(i) An act is morally right only because authority P holds it is morally right.
(ii) Authority P holds an act is morally right only on the basis of those features which really do make it morally right.

Set 2

(i) An act is morally right for a person only because that person believes it is morally right for him.
(ii) The person in (i) believes the act is morally right for him solely on the basis of those features which really do make it morally right for him.

Set 3

(i) An act is morally right only because it proceeds from a morally good (or 'sincere'?) motivation.
(ii) An act's proceeding from a morally good (or sincere) motivation requires that the act be prompted to some extent by one's belief that the act is morally right.
(iii) The belief in (ii) is formed solely with regard to those features which do make it right, i.e. those given in (i).

Set 4

(i) An act is morally right for me only because I will it, given that

(ii) I will the act because I (already) believe it is morally right, where

(iii) My belief that the act is morally right is based solely on (i).

Set 5

(i) An act is morally right only because the law (or social opinion) requires that act.

(ii) The law (or social opinion) requires that act on the grounds that it is already morally right, where

(iii) The grounds cited are specifically those in (i).

Set 6

(i) A policy alternative is morally right simply because the majority voted for it.

(ii) Everyone in the majority voted for the alternative solely on the basis of the belief that it was (already) morally right, where

(iii) All such beliefs were based solely on correct applications of (i).

Set 7

(i) Acts are immoral because and only because they cause harm to others.

(ii) But in some cases where acts are wrong the harm to other persons consists solely in the moral sensibilities of those others being offended, where

(iii) Those moral sensibilities involve no other moral beliefs than that in (i).

Set 8

(i) Something is morally valuable for a person only because that person values it in the moral way.

(ii) A person values something in the moral way only because that person first believes it is morally valuable, where

(iii) The belief in (ii) that something is morally valuable is based solely on the criterion given in (i).

Set 9

(i) x is good for me just because I desire x.
(ii) I desire x precisely because I already think x good.

FURTHER READING

Basic discussions of theistic ethics can be found in Brandt (1959: ch. 4) and Hospers (1961: 29–34). An interesting dissent from these standard views is in Williams (1972: 77–86). For a more advanced discussion see Helm (1981).

Further comment on *Euthyphro* can be found in Cohen (1971) and Geach (1972). The Euthyphro problem in set 9 above is discussed with some unexpected and interesting twists in Wiggins (1976: 348); see also Griffin (1986: 26–31).

Among the important historical theistic philosophers the following are usually held to be anti-voluntarists: Thomas Aquinas, Ralph Cudworth, Henry More, Samuel Clarke. While clear voluntarists are somewhat harder to find, William of Occam seems a likely candidate. Discussions of Aquinas and Occam can be found in Copleston's history of philosophy (1963). Selections from Cudworth, More, and Clarke can be found in Selby-Bigge (1897).

3

Some classic ethical theories

SOME KINDS OF MORAL AND VALUE JUDGEMENTS

The main normative kinds of ethical theories discussed by philosophers have been neither authoritarian nor subjectivist. Thus they do not seem subject to Socrates' Euthyphro objection. However, before we examine some examples of such theories we need to distinguish some of the main kinds of moral and value judgements. Chapter 1 indicated some of the variety of moral judgements we make in everyday life. Among this variety, there seem to be some particularly important main kinds (Frankena 1973: 9–10, 80–3). While these may not be the only kinds (and even these may overlap somewhat), distinguishing and understanding these kinds of judgements is important for understanding the ethical theories which are the subject of this chapter.

1 Moral rightness judgements: judgements to guide choice

One kind of moral judgement is directly addressed to decision-making problems. The nature of this sort of judgement can be seen most clearly in situations where one has yet to choose a course of action and one raises the question what, if anything, morality requires in just that situation. Again, someone may come to you for moral advice about a choice to be made. Your prescription, or advice, would be an example of this sort of moral judgement.

Such judgements typically employ not only the term 'right' but other terms such as 'obligation', 'ought', 'duty', 'is to be done', and 'should'. Other frequently used terms are readily definable in

31

terms of 'right' or 'ought', e.g. 'wrong' (=$_{df}$ 'ought not to do') and 'permissible' (=$_{df}$ 'not ought not to do'). However, we should not suppose that these terms invariably are used to make judgements falling under our first category. First, such terms can also figure in many *non-moral* value judgements. For instance, there are merely prudential and 'technical' uses of 'ought', e.g. 'You really ought to insure your house contents' (presumably you are just foolish, rather than immoral, if you don't). Second, sometimes the above terms are used to make *moral* judgements of other kinds than the present sort. For example, the judgement that a person has committed 'a wrong' is very probably a judgement of the next sort to be discussed.

2 Virtue judgements: assessing persons and performances

Some moral judgements assess persons overall, or assess certain aspects of their character (their virtues, dispositions, habits, traits), or they may assess them more particularly in regard to their performance on a particular occasion. Even in regard to a particular performance, questions of the person's motives, intentions, dispositions and habits, willpower, degree of control, degree of responsibility for the performance, etc. are of importance in assessing the manner in which the agent acted. A rather important concern in that regard is whether the agent did what he did 'deliberately', 'knowingly', 'inadvertently', 'negligently', or whatever. Questions of the agent's responsibility or liability are especially important when assessing such things as the reward, punishment, praise, or blame appropriate to his performance. Judgements assessing persons and their performances, unlike judgements of sort (1), are most appropriately raised *after* the act has been performed.

Judgements of moral goodness of persons and performances are not to be confused with judgements of the rightness or wrongness of the course of action chosen. A morally *right act* (i.e. one we would prescribe to anyone in exactly such a choice situation) can be performed by a *bad person* and even be a *bad act* (e.g. if done only because the agent thought he could gain the most for himself). Likewise a *wrong act* can be done by a *good person* and not be a *bad act* (e.g. if done unwittingly, unintentionally, or by mistake). A person is not always responsible for his wrong, or even his right, acts.

Some people like to make morality seem more 'subjective' (whatever exactly that means!) than it is. They say such things as 'Any act could be right or wrong; morality is all a matter of motives and intentions, hence subjective'. This just seems to be confusing moral goodness (or badness) of performance, (2), with moral rightness (or wrongness) of courses of action, (1). Of course a *wrong* act does not inevitably turn out to be a *bad* one (in the sense that the agent (i.e. 'subject') is to be assessed as 'bad' or 'responsible' for doing wrong). But while assessing the moral performance of agents in their action may involve bringing in their motives and intentions, it does not follow that the rightness or wrongness of the course chosen depends on any such 'subjective' element. The above is a good example of how certain seemingly sophisticated attitudes are based on nothing more than that kind of confusion which a little philosophy and reflection can avoid.

Some moral philosophers (e.g. Immanuel Kant, or the Stoics) have supposed that judgements of moral goodness of persons (e.g. judgements about 'virtue' and the 'morally good will') are of central importance in morality. Some contemporary philosophers go even further. They don't just emphasize virtue, they typically hold that the place to *begin* moral philosophy is with virtue judgements. By contrast, many classic ethical theories begin with rightness, and only develop a theory of virtue later, on the basis of the theory of rightness. And this raises an important issue of priority. Some philosophers have thought it plausible that judgements of moral rightness are *logically prior* to judgements of moral goodness of agents. They have thought, for example, that the 'definition' or 'analysis' of moral goodness of agents would involve, perhaps among other conditions, a disposition to perform an act because it is morally right. On this view the notion of moral rightness of acts is logically prior to that of moral goodness of agents, in that the latter notion already involves the former (which is 'more primitive', as philosophers say). However, if this were so, it would not be possible to turn around and attempt to define or analyse moral rightness by employing the notion of moral goodness. For example, one could not then suppose that to say an act is 'morally right' just means it was 'willed by a *morally good* will' or 'was done out of a morally good intention'. For that would make moral goodness, in turn, logically prior to moral rightness. If one is going to explain moral goodness in terms of moral rightness, one cannot then explain moral rightness in terms of moral goodness. Indeed we can put the above in terms of a Euthyphro dilemma:

(i) 'A is morally *right*' =$_{df}$ 'A was done from a morally *good* intention.'

(ii) 'A was done from a morally *good* intention' =$_{df}$ '. . .& A was done because it was believed that A is morally *right*.'

To hold both (i) and (ii) at once takes us in a definitional circle. Moral theories that give priority to rightness judgements (obligation moralities) will reject any general account of rightness that builds on judgements of virtues. Hence we expect such theories to reject (i). They may or may not accept (ii). On the other hand, moral theories that give priority to virtue judgements (virtue moralities) will reject any general account of virtue that presupposes rightness. Hence (ii) will be rejected as a general account of moral virtue. Such a theory might instead emphasize motives, habits, and dispositions other than the sheer regard to moral rightness, e.g. benevolent concern for others, loathing of the infliction of harm, concern for one's offspring.

3 Judgements of well-being

A great many of these judgements would not seem to be *moral* judgements at all, although they are still *value* (or normative) judgements. Of course this does not mean they are *im*moral or *a*moral. They are just not moral judgements. (Aesthetic judgements would be another example of normative, but not moral, judgements.) There are many everyday examples of this sort of judgement. I speak of 'a good day', 'a good feeling', 'a good meal', 'a good time', 'a person's own good'. Ancient philosophers like to speak of 'the good life'. Or you might say 'A swim would be good now'. In most of these cases 'good' does not mean 'moral'. (Indeed some good feelings and good times are to be had in immoral ways.) Admittedly some philosophers have given accounts of human well-being which bring in notions of moral ideals or moral virtues. But a great many others have not. Typically, philosophers connect the nature of a person's good with what promotes one's welfare, benefit, happiness, interest, or with what it is prudent or expedient or advantageous for one to do. Not surprisingly, such judgements of well-being are person-relative. What is in your interest may not always be in mine. A medicine which cures you might kill me. One might wonder what such judgements have to do with moral philosophy. We will take that up shortly.

4 Ideals and values

This sort of judgement, unlike (3), is clearly a *moral* assessment. However, unlike (2), it is not concerned with assessing individuals, their motivations, their responsibility, and liability. Furthermore, unlike (1), it is not in the first instance concerned with prescriptions for choice (even if such judgements can sometimes have implications in that regard). For example, one might judge it a morally good state of affairs that society has certain traditions of toleration, or respect for civil liberties, or a high degree of culture. Or we may assess certain social structures or traditions in terms of their justice, stability, or efficiency. Again, it may be that the existence of certain kinds of human relationships is thought to be a good thing. This sort of moral assessment *needn't* have any direct connection with any prescriptions addressed to individuals. For example, one might think there is nothing much individuals can do in regard to social structures and traditions. Such things might be, to some extent, just moral good luck.

The categories (1) through (4) do not exhaust the kinds of value (normative) judgements that there are, and may even not exhaust the kinds of moral judgements there are. Furthermore, many important questions arise in regard to what relations hold between the different kinds of judgements. But a more immediate question is why category (3) gets on our list in the first place. After all, judgements of non-moral good do not even pretend to be moral judgements. Why should such a judgement ever get into a discussion of moral philosophy?

There are perhaps two answers to this. First, what the ancient Greeks called 'ethics' seems to have been in the first instance concerned with judgements about what is 'the good for humans'. Moral rightness, (1), and moral goodness, (2), do get into the picture, however. Plato, Aristotle, the Stoics, and some others tried to give arguments to show that the non-morally good life involves, as an essential ingredient, moral virtue or goodness. Being morally good, they thought, was an essential ingredient in the (non-morally) good life. Thus they tried to solve problem P4 of chapter 1 by giving arguments that there was no ultimate conflict between duty ('being just') and true self-interest ('advantage').

But some more modern moral philosophers need to discuss well-being for a quite different reason. One sort of normative ethics brings *well-being* into the account of what makes acts *morally* right. One such view is that acts are morally right *because* of the well-being they produce. This might well seem a plausible thing to say once one has rejected a theistically based normative ethics. If moral rightness does not rest on God's commands, why not then suppose rightness is a matter of maximizing something like total social happiness or welfare (i.e. human non-moral good)? This looks both benevolent and down-to-earth.

TELEOLOGICAL ETHICAL THEORIES

Such normative ethical theories are usually called 'teleological'. Of course a lot of different ethical theories count as teleological ones. What teleological theories have in common is that they all claim that acts are morally right because (and only because) of the well-being thereby produced (and the 'evils' avoided). Moral rightness is thus a matter of 'consequences', but not just any consequences. Only one kind of consequence is relevant, viz. the amount of good, i.e. well-being, produced. Any teleological normative ethics will thus have to go on to specify two further things:

First, a teleologist must specify the nature of the non-moral good. Some have identified it with pleasure sensations, others with happiness, others with fame or success, others with moral virtue, others with certain human relationships, others with aesthetic experiences, others with a mystical experience such as 'the vision of God', and so on. Of course you need not be a teleologist in ethics to have views on the good life or on human well-being. But teleologists *must* have views on this for their normative ethics to issue in any conclusions about what acts are morally right.

Second, a teleologist must specify *whose* good or well-being. One's own? A certain group's? Everyone's? Is the teleologist saying 'An act is morally right *for everyone* if it maximizes *my* welfare'? (Such people must think they are God, or very special.) Or, is the teleologist saying 'An act is morally right for a given person if it maximizes that very person's welfare?' This somewhat more impartial view is sometimes called 'impersonal ethical egoism'. (Question: Is it really in the interest of impersonal ethical egoists to go about propagating their view?) Or is the teleologist saying, 'An act is morally right if it maximizes the well-being of [say] the Aryan race?' Or of the corporation? Or of the proletariat? Or, finally, is the teleologist saying 'An act is morally right if it maximizes the welfare of *everyone*'? In the latter case the person would be a *universal* teleologist.

One leading kind of universal teleologist is the utilitarian. The most typical kind of utilitarian identifies well-being ('utility') with something like happiness or pleasure. ('Ideal' utilitarians such as Moore (1903) identify well-being with one's realizing certain ideals.) Utilitarianism of this typical sort has had a rather good run in philosophical circles in the nineteenth and twentieth centuries (e.g. J. Bentham, J.S. Mill, and, more recently, J.J.C. Smart). Utilitarians hold that an act is morally right because it produces the greatest balance of happiness (or welfare) for society as a whole (compared with all its alternatives). For the utilitarian an act is morally right *because* of certain social consequences it has (i.e. happiness produced and unhappiness prevented). Thus if it is right to punish criminals, this cannot be because of what lies in the past (e.g. their past criminal acts or intentions), but must be because of what consequences punishment will produce (e.g. deterrence, prevention, reform).

Utilitarianism has both its plausibility and its problems. Its basic plausibility lies in the notion of rationality it employs, and its social point of view. At the level of individual choice the principle of rationality that many find plausible is to maximize expected utility. Add to this the claim that moral judgements take the social point of view rather than the individual point of view and it is natural to slide to the conclusion that moral rightness is a matter of maximizing the expected utility, not of some individual, but of society.

DEONTOLOGICAL ETHICAL THEORIES

A deontologist in normative ethics is anyone who is not a teleologist. An extreme deontologist would deny that the goodness produced by an act had *anything* to do with its moral rightness. The more usual deontological view is that the goodness produced by an act is sometimes *relevant to* its moral rightness but *is not the sole determinant* of moral rightness. An act can be right for other reasons than the welfare it brings about. Typically deontologists mention features which have to do with the past (e.g. the act was one you promis*ed*), or else they cite features having nothing to do with the non-moral good produced, such as one's present role or relationships to others (e.g. the mere relationship of 'being a parent' might be thought to give rise to certain obligations).

Ross and prima-facie rules

A rather clear example of a deontological normative ethics is to be found in the views of the early twentieth–century philosopher W.D. Ross. Ross did not think that all our ordinary everyday moral judgements could be formulated adequately in terms of some single rule or principle from which they could all be derived. Instead, he thought a theory adequate to our everyday practice would come in the form of a *set* of rules (of a sort). In *The Right and the Good* (Ross 1930:21) he lists the following main kinds of duties.

  (i) Duties which rest on one's own previous acts (e.g., a duty to keep a promise, the duty to make reparation for a past wrongful act).
 (ii) Duties which rest on previous acts of others (e.g., duties of gratitude for past services).
(iii) Duties of justice (i.e., the duty to prevent or upset distributions of pleasure or happiness not based on the merit of persons).
(iv) Duties of beneficence (i.e., to improve the conditions of others).
 (v) Duties of self-improvement.
(vi) The duty not to injure others.

Now duties of sorts (iv)–(vi) *might* be construed as based on the non-moral good which can be produced. If Ross's set of rules consisted of only these, his theory would look rather teleological. But duties of sorts (i)–(iii) are sufficient to prevent his theory from being teleological. For example, the duty in (i) to keep a promise is not based on the amount of non-moral good keeping a promise might produce. (There might *also* be a duty to increase non-moral good – as in (iv) – but that is not what (i) is based on.)

An obvious problem for any ethics in the form of a set of rules is problem P1 in chapter 1, i.e. the problem of internal conflicts. What if, for example, the duty to keep a promise conflicts with the duty to improve oneself? Or with the duty not to injure others? It is in response to this problem that Ross developed the notion of a prima-facie rule. The rule in (i) to keep your promises is only a prima-facie rule, not an *absolute* one. The feature of 'having promised to do this act' is, Ross says, a *duty-making* property. He explains what this means thus: First, when an act falls under a prima-facie rule such as (i), i.e. has the duty-making property therein mentioned, and when the omission of that act falls under no other prima-facie rule (i.e. the omission has no duty-making feature), there is then an *overall* duty to do the act (e.g. keep the promise). But, second, when an act and its omission each fall under different duties (i.e. both have different duty-making properties), the act may or may not then be an *overall* duty. That will depend on which is the 'weightier' duty. For example, normally the duty to keep a promise is weightier than the duty to improve oneself but not as weighty as the duty not to kill.

But this means Ross's moral system is not complete with just a set of prima-facie rules. He also needs something like a set of second-order rules to determine the cases where the first-order (prima-facie) rules conflict. However, it is not at all implausible that something like a set of prima-facie rules with some second-order procedures for deciding first-order conflicts is implicitly behind the everyday moral judgements we make. Ross's theory might be adequate as a *formulation* of the implicit moral principles behind our everyday judgements. Of course problems P3 and P4 in chapter 1 may lead us to ask whether our implicit conventional moral principles are *justified*. (In chapter 12 we pursue this question further.)

Kant's categorical imperative

Kant's famous categorical imperative is not really a rule for determining moral right and wrong. Rather, it is a rule for determining the rules of morality. It is a rule-generating rule. Kant states the categorical imperative thus: 'Act only according to that maxim by which you can at the same time will that it should become a universal law.' A 'maxim' is a bit like a rule, although it need not be a moral rule. For example, a rational decision to perform a certain act typically, perhaps inevitably, presupposes a particular reason (or reasons) for doing that act: 'I should do act A because feature F is present', where this is equivalent to a rule 'The presence of F in any act is some reason for doing that act', or 'May I do acts where F is present (other things being equal)' or 'Prima facie, I should do F-sort acts'. A 'maxim' is any judgement a person makes about what is a good reason for (i.e. a right-making feature of) *his* acting, or not acting, in a certain way.

Now one interpretation of Kant's categorical imperative is as follows (see Frankena 1973: 30–3): A 'maxim' will give an actual moral duty if and only if both of two further conditions are met:

(i) One can consistently will a social system where *everyone* accepts and operates on that maxim.

(ii) One cannot consistently will a social system where *everyone* rejects and does not operate on that maxim.

For example, Kant thinks one can consistently will a society which operates on a maxim such as 'Keep your promises', or a maxim requiring one to give aid or show concern for others, at least in certain circumstances. However, Kant thinks one cannot consistently will a system where these maxims are rejected by *everyone*, in favour of maxims such as 'Keep your promise only if you want to' or 'Think only of yourself'.

Kant seems to have intended 'can will' in a particularly strong sense. It was not for him a matter of what one's peculiar psychological nature is capable of accepting. Rather, he seems to have been concerned with cases where what is willed involves some conceptual absurdity, or an essentially self-defeating state of affairs. It is a matter of what one can *consistently* will. For example, a society where everyone (openly!) operated on the maxim 'Keep a promise only if it suits you' is not merely an inconvenient or undesirable one, it is conceptually absurd and essentially self-defeating. (What would the strange ceremony of uttering 'I promise . . .' *mean*? What would be its point? Would it even *be* promising in such a context?)

Many moral philosophers, who might reject other things in Kant, accept something like condition (i) as a necessary, though not sufficient, condition of a moral maxim. They claim that to think morally is to look at questions of action from a social point of view. If a judgement about a particular person is to be a *moral* one (rather than merely prudential, aesthetic, or evaluative in some other way), it presupposes a rule which is to apply to *anyone* in such circumstances. (I may be the promisee or the debtor today, but tomorrow, when I am the promiser or the creditor, the *same rule*, whatever it is, must apply.) R.M. Hare, an important twentieth–century moral philosopher, claims that any *moral* judgement has to be 'universalizable' in some such way.

Condition (ii) fits somewhat with our ordinary moral thinking. Many acts ordinarily considered morally wrong might be considered as the acts of a social parasite. This is the person who breaks promises on a whim, or assaults, or steals, or who gets a video recorder at a greatly reduced price from someone who got it 'off the back of a truck'. But at the same time he expects (i.e. 'wills') that others keep their promises to him, that society and the law protect him from assault and theft. He is outraged when his own flat is burgled and ransacked. He lives by a set of maxims he would not (perhaps, could not) want society as a whole to live by.

In summary, utilitarianism (of various forms) and, perhaps, ethical egoism provide the main examples of teleological theories. Ross's theory and Kant's theory are two (among many) examples of deontological theory. (I leave it to you to consider *why* Kant's theory is deontological.)

FURTHER READING

For general treatments of the matters discussed in this chapter, see Frankena (1973: chs 1, 2, 3, 5), Brandt (1959: chs 12, 13), Prichard (1912: esp. 5–7), and Louden (1984). Louden contains further references on virtue-based ethical theories.

Useful histories of ethical theories include Broad (1930), MacIntyre (1966), and Sidgwick (1886).

On ethical egoism, see Brandt (1959: ch. 14, sec. 2, 369–75; see also the references listed on 379), Brandt (1979: 267–70), Frankena (1973: 17–20), Hospers (1961: sec. 10, 157–74), Medlin (1957), Regis (1980), and Williams (1973: 250–65).

Among the main primary works on utilitarianism are Bentham (1780: chs 1, 2, 3, 4, 10), Mill (1861), Moore (1903), and Smart and Williams (1973). These present a secular utilitarianism; for examples of theological utilitarianism see Gay (1731) and Paley (1785).

Classic primary works in the deontological tradition are Ross (1930) and Kant (1785).

For ancient Greek ethics see Plato's *Republic* and Aristotle's *Nichomachean Ethics*. Useful secondary sources are MacIntyre (1966: chs 1–7) and Adkins (1960).

4

Psychological egoism and hedonism

At the beginning of chapter 2 a distinction was made between what it is that *justifies* a certain course of action and what it is that actually *motivates* a particular person to so act in a given case. But while normative questions of justification are not to be just confused outright with descriptive questions about motivation, there may still be some important relationships between motivations and justifications (i.e. between psychological questions and moral questions). Very few moral philosophers, if any, have denied that facts about human nature and, specifically, human motivation bear on moral philosophy in various important ways.

THE MEANINGS OF THE TWO THESES

Two psychological theses about motivation have sometimes been put forward as having particularly important, perhaps disastrous, consequences for moral philosophy. These are psychological egoism and psychological hedonism. *Psychological egoism* (PE) is the thesis that each person is motivated, ultimately, *only* by self-interest (alternatively: selfish desires). According to this theory one might on occasion do things which are in the interests of others, but in every case this will be only *as a means* to one's own self-interest. In such cases one can be said to desire the well-being of others, but only as a means to one's own well-being. According to the psychological egoist, the only thing one desires *as an end* (or, for itself) is one's own self-interest. *Psychological hedonism* (PH) is the thesis that each person is motivated, ultimately, *only* by the desire for his own pleasure (understood as including the aversion to pain). One could be a psychological egoist without being a psychological hedonist, provided one had a notion of 'self-interest' that included more than just maximization of the balance of pleasure over pain for oneself (or a notion of 'selfish' that could apply to other desires than the desires to get pleasure and avoid pain for oneself). For example, such a psychological egoist might hold that success of some sort was an important ingredient in self-interest (or that the desire for success was selfish), but without thinking that success had to be regarded merely as something one desires as a means to pleasurable sensations and experiences. Hence, psychological egoism does not automatically entail psychological hedonism. On the other hand, psychological hedonism looks like it should be an instance of psychological egoism. The desire for *one's own* pleasure looks like a sufficiently selfish motivation to count as egoistic.

Psychological egoism and psychological hedonism are motivational, and hence psychological, theses. They are descriptive in the sense that they try to describe what it is that always motivates people. These descriptive theses are not to be confused with the following normative ethical theories:

(a) *Ethical* egoism: the normative ethical theory that the only feature making one's act right is its maximizing one's own self-interest (in comparison with the other acts available).
(b) *Ethical* hedonism: the normative ethical theory that the only feature making one's act right is its maximizing the balance of pleasure over pain for oneself (in comparison with the other acts available).

Each of the above ethical theses claims that a certain feature and only that feature can justify acting. Both theses claim to give the sole grounds relevant to the issue of how one ought to act. By contrast *psychological* egoism and *psychological* hedonism claim to describe how we actually do act and what motivates us. They say that we do act in these ways, not necessarily that we should.

Perhaps it is even too strong to say they are theories about how we do act. The psychological egoist does not have to claim that each individual will always do the act which is the most in his self-interest. It must be very rare that one is so lucky as to do just that. At best, he will say, one does the act one *believes* is most in his own self-interest. But a psychological egoist doesn't even have to say that. Most psychological egoists admit that we can fail to do even what we believe to be most in our own self-interest, because of such things as weakness of will, irrationality, etc. But even in those sorts of cases, the psychological egoist will insist that all of our desires are selfish or self-interested ones, even if these do not always lead us to act in the optimally self-interested manner. Likewise a psychological hedonist doesn't have to say we will always do the act which in fact will maximize our own pleasure-over-pain balance, or even that we will always do the act we believe has this feature. But he will say that all the motivations we have are either desires for pleasure and the avoidance of pain or else are desires for the means to these things. There are no other motivations not reducible to these.

Psychological egoism and hedonism are not quite the same as certain *genetic* theses with which they are sometimes associated:

(c) Egoistic *genetic* thesis (EGT): all of our present motivations as individuals (alternative: as a species) arose originally out of self-interested or selfish desires.

(d) Hedonistic *genetic* thesis (HGT): all of our present motivations as individuals (alternative: as a species) arose originally out of desires for pleasure and the avoidance of pain.

EGT does not automatically prove PE, nor does HGT automatically prove PH. To suppose that the genetic thesis proves the corresponding psychological thesis about our present-day motivations is one version of the so-called 'genetic fallacy'. (A somewhat different alleged fallacy going under the name 'genetic fallacy' is discussed in chapters 8 and 9.) The fallacy consists in supposing that in all such cases a thing *must* have the same nature as its original cause, or that in all cases a thing *must* have the same nature as it did at an earlier stage. But even if a desire I now have originally was acquired by, say, a schedule of reinforcement with pleasure and pain sensations, it does not automatically follow that the desire I have now is really only *for* pleasure and pain avoidance. Likewise, that a desire might have originated from a learning process involving an initial reliance on selfish desires does not automatically show that the desire which has developed is a desire for such things. (Cf. the useful discussion of 'functional autonomy' in Slote (1964).)

Finally, it should be noticed that both psychological egoism and psychological hedonism are quite extreme theses. They are not merely saying that there is a lot of selfishness and hedonism about (a great deal more than the naïve suppose). They are claiming that, quite without exception, the other kinds of motivation do not (or cannot) occur. If either of these theories is true, it would be quite pointless to bemoan the fact that pure altruism (i.e. an act done not just as a means to self-interest or pleasure) is rare. These theories don't say that it is rare but that it is nonexistent, and that bemoaning this fact is particularly pointless because it is psychologically impossible for it to be otherwise.

THE RELEVANCE TO ETHICAL THEORY

Both psychological egoism and psychological hedonism have been thought consequential for normative ethical theory by various philosophers. But in fact they have been thought consequential in several different sorts of ways. I will list three of these ways:

1 The theory of the non-moral good

Some philosophers have taken one or the other of these psychological theses to bear on the (normative) issue of what is one's non-moral good. A typical, but controversial, kind of view about non-moral goodness is that what is one's non-moral good is a function of, or is determined by, one's desires. What is non-morally good for you must depend in some way on what you desire, or at any rate on what you can desire. Let us call any such view a 'desire-based theory of the non-moral good'. If some such theory is right, then the truth of either psychological egoism or psychological hedonism would have implications for what is in fact to one's non-moral good. For example, someone who accepted a desire-based theory of the non-moral good and who also thought psychological hedonism was a correct account of human nature might reason thus:

(i) Desire-based theory of the non-moral good: what is one's non-moral good is completely determined by what it is that one does (or perhaps, can) desire.

(ii) Psychological hedonism: one desires, and can desire, only pleasure for oneself.

Therefore

(iii) Pleasure is the (sole) non-moral good for a person.

Naturally such a result would be of particular importance for teleological ethical theories. Some utilitarians may have held something like this.

2 The 'ought' implies 'can' thesis

A common, even if controversial and somewhat obscure, thesis in the philosophical literature is encapsulated in the formula ' "ought" implies "can" '. In fact there are a number of theses caught by this notoriously ambiguous formula. Here are two of the more important interpretations:

(i) Where one cannot do an action, it is pointless and inappropriate to raise the issue of whether one *ought* to do that action.

(ii) If a person *could not* have acted otherwise, it is inappropriate to *blame* that person for having done what he did.

Even in each of these two cases there will be several importantly different interpretations depending on what kinds of impossibility or incapacity the 'cannot' (or 'could not') is taken to cover. Let's choose the interpretations which cover what we might call motivational incapacity. Notice that if (i), interpreted in that way, is true, and if psychological egoism is also true, it will follow that it is pointless and inappropriate to raise the question of whether one should do an act where there is no self-interested motivation that could ever lead one to do that act. Likewise, if the motivational version of (ii) is true, and if psychological egoism is also true, then it will be inappropriate to blame a person for not acting out of some motive other than an egoistic one. Psychological egoism holds that no one *can* act from any other motive.

3 The theory of sanctions

If psychological egoism or psychological hedonism is true, it would seem to follow that many of the ethical theories we have discussed – particularly those in chapter 3 – have an implementation problem. Merely recognizing the moral rightness of acts, in accordance with one of those ethical theories, could not, according to psychological egoism and hedonism, provide any motivation at all. Even if the correct theory of morality is to be found in, say, Ross or Kant, merely knowing the truth of such a theory will avail little if we can only be motivated egoistically or hedonistically. Even a moral theory such as utilitarianism, which is concerned to maximize happiness, or desire satisfaction, or balance of pleasures over pains, is concerned to do this generally, i.e. over society as a whole. But a concern for the *general* happiness is not a motivation the psychological egoist or hedonist allows (except where this is desired as a means to one's own self-interest or pleasure).

Utilitarians who are also psychological egoists (or hedonists) typically meet this motivational problem with a theory of sanctions. Society's and the state's attaching various pleasures and pains to certain acts can motivate individuals to act for the general welfare when they would not otherwise be motivated to do so. Examples of 'sanctions' in the legal system are tax incentives on the one hand and fines and punishments on the other. Examples of 'sanctions' in the social system are praise and blame. A crude version of the theory of sanctions argues that since humans are motivated only by rewards and punishments (or pleasures and pains), it is pointless to try other means of social control such as moral argument, or moral education. More sophisticated versions (e.g. Bentham, Mill, Smart) emphasize the motivating sanctions of social pressure. Indeed they regard the role of many moral judgements (especially judgements of moral goodness and badness, of responsibility, guilt, etc.) as being to motivate those thereby praised or blamed. Finally, the most sophisticated versions of the theory of sanctions emphasize the 'inner sanctions' of conscience and moral belief. Of course the psychological egoist or hedonist who allows moral motivation as a sanction must then give some account of moral motivation, reducing it to self-interest or the desire for pleasure and the aversion to pain. (Can this be done?)

For these three reasons, then, it might seem rather pointless to proceed with the discussion of ethical theories (and justifying reasons) until we determine whether either psychological egoism or psychological hedonism is true. If either is true, we may not need to consider a great many ethical theories any further. We will take up psychological egoism first, leaving the special case of psychological hedonism to later in this chapter.

BUTLER'S REFUTATION OF PSYCHOLOGICAL EGOISM

Joseph Butler's refutation of psychological egoism is one of those classic, set pieces of philosophical reasoning which every student of philosophy should know. In that respect it is in the same category as Socrates' Euthyphro argument (discussed in chapter 2) and Socrates' Theaetetus argument against Protagoras' relativistic views (discussed in chapter 7). As with Socrates' two arguments, Butler's argument is not the last word on the subject addressed, but it is certainly the first word. Each of these three set piece arguments has the result of turning the tables on a certain rather glib philosophical view, putting it on the defensive. After Butler's refutation there would still be reasonable defences of psychological egoism (see Slote 1964), but the starting point of these defences would always be a reply to Butler. After Butler, just as after Socrates, things could never be quite the same again.

What I shall describe as 'Butler's refutation' is not an entirely accurate historical description of Butler's views. Instead I use that phrase to describe an argument that begins with Butler (1726) but which has been refined and revised by a number of philosophers such as Broad (1930, 1949–50) and Feinberg (1975). So I will really be discussing what has become of Butler's argument – the Butler tradition, one might say.

What Butler's argument tries to prove

It might seem odd that a descriptive thesis about human nature could be allegedly refuted, armchair-fashion, by a philosophical argument such as Butler's. After all, Butler's argument is not a matter of gaining any new evidence or even proposing any new scientific hypotheses. However, I think this will seem not quite so odd if we see that the psychological egoism toward which Butler's argument is directed is itself something of an armchair thesis. That is, the psychological egoism in question is not, as it might first present itself, based on any new scientific evidence or theory. Part of the effect of Butler's argument is to expose a great many psychological egoists as really doing nothing more than engaging in a lot of deceptive labelling.

This brings us to the nature of Butler's accusation against psychological egoism. (This is not Butler's argument yet, only the accusation, i.e. the conclusion toward which the argument works.) One thing the Butler argument would like to show is that psychological egoism is often nothing more than just a determination to use words like 'selfish' or 'self-interest' in new, misleading ways, with the consequence that 'selfish' or 'self-interested' no longer can be used to mark the rather useful distinctions which they did before redefinition. It's important to get clear about the nature of this accusation. (We can examine the argument for it afterwards.) In this regard we might consider other sorts of cases where we might *suspect*, at least, that what is being put forward as a provocative philosophical thesis is really nothing more than a ruining of the work of an otherwise perfectly useful ordinary term.

Consider that rather tedious sort of person who thinks he is introducing us to some deeper level of insight when he says such things as 'No cup is ever really *full*', or perhaps, 'No surface is ever really *flat*'. These are not people who have made any measurements we have not, or who base their statements on particular observations not generally known. Their 'discoveries' are put forth from the armchair. And indeed certain philosophical theses are rather like this as well, and may be suspect for the same reason, e.g. 'Nothing is ever certain', 'There is never a case of knowledge', 'Everything is relative', as well as some currently trendy aphorisms, such as: 'All statements are really political, i.e. ideological', 'Every text has a (political or ideological) subtext', 'Everything is literature, e.g. postage stamps, postcards', 'All assertions make social (hiss!) assumptions'. Some philosophers have argued that we could not have learned words like 'flat' or 'know' except by having them applied to certain instances and denied to contrasting instances, and that therefore such words derive their meanings from these contrasts, and hence that such a word cannot be used meaningfully to deny the very contrast that gives it meaning. Most contemporary philosophers now think that these arguments go too far. But, while it is perhaps just barely *possible* that such sweeping claims can be true, they are nevertheless very *suspect* claims. We may reasonably *suspect* that all that is going on is a determination to use an old word in a new way, with the consequence that a rather useful distinction can no longer be marked by its use (although the speaker may succeed in appearing rather provocative and profound).

We might examine in more detail a particular case, one that isn't loaded with philosophical controversy. Consider again the claim of the tedious person who says 'Nothing is really flat'. The first thing we should note is that 'flat' in this claim is being employed out of all contexts. Normally 'flat' gets its standard of application determined by its context. For example, 'flat' in regard to floors assumes one context. 'Flat' in regard to terrain, or stomachs, or precision tools, assumes quite different contexts. In normal use the standard of flatness is different in different contexts. What is flat for terrain (e.g. the Nullarbor Plain) would not be flat for a precision tool. But the tedious person who says 'Nothing is flat' uses 'flat' out of all contexts. And, second, he at the same time ups the standard impossibly high, so high that nothing will pass the test. This, of course, is all done in the armchair. But the result is that the word 'flat', which formerly had a number of useful employments, in various contexts, is no longer of any real use at all. Indeed, in so far as we are tempted to suppose the *old* sense of 'flat' is still being employed, the sweeping claim made in the *new* sense is wildly misleading. It suggests that the Nullarbor is really in there with the Snowy Mountains, that we are all obese, and that we may as well throw away all our precision tools. It suggests that there are no important differences in degree. But of course there are. The grocer who short-sells us cannot expect a court to accept as his excuse 'No carton is ever full'. Some are fuller than others. (However, we are more likely to be taken in by the trendy academic who says 'All assertions are political anyway' as his excuse for inflicting on us his own unabashed piece of political propaganda.) Finally, we should notice that the tedious person who says 'Nothing is flat' has no new observational or theoretical basis for his claim, no reason for rushing out to change the geological survey maps or to institute a new national health programme or to rectify industrial standards. All he really has to offer us is a rather pointless linguistic proposal. He proposes to stretch the meaning of 'flat' so that it no longer can be used to make any useful distinction or mark any useful contrast.

Something like this is what the Butler argument accuses the psychological egoist of doing in regard to 'selfish' or 'self-interested'. It accuses the psychological egoist of having no real psychological thesis to offer but only a rather pointless, and misleading, linguistic recommendation. Butler accuses the psychological egoist of accomplishing no more than the rendering useless of words which up to that point were used to mark quite useful distinctions. That's the accusation. What's the argument?

Stage 1: The refutation of extreme psychological egoism

The Butler argument has two stages. Stage 1 is Butler's argument against *extreme* psychological egoism. Stage 2 is Butler's argument against *moderate* psychological egoism. Stage 1 may not seem very important at first glance, because moderate psychological egoism is by far the more plausible thesis. But when he forces a psychological egoist to abandon the extreme version in favour of the moderate version, Butler thereby extracts an innocent-looking concession which is in fact crucial in Butler's argument at stage 2, the argument against moderate psychological egoism. Hence stage 1 must be discussed before stage 2.

The *extreme psychological egoist* holds that there is really only one principle of human motivation, viz. 'self-love', to use the eighteenth-century term, or 'self-interest', to use the more contemporary term. The extreme psychological egoist may also allow as motivationally relevant something Butler calls 'reason'. But 'reason' has a rather restricted sense here. It is a matter of calculating means toward ends. The psychological egoist does not think of 'reason' as being an independent motivational principle that might come into conflict with self-interest. Reason is only a tool of self-interest (self-love).

We might note that the extreme version of psychological egoism has a couple of odd consequences. First, while the extreme psychological egoist can allow that we do have a lot of desires for particular objects at particular times (e.g. for beer, or applause, or money, or sexual pleasure), these things must be desired, never just for themselves, but only as a *means* to the one thing the extreme psychological egoist thinks we desire for itself, i.e. our own self-interest. The second odd feature of psychological egoism is as follows. The extreme view is that the ultimate principle of motivation is *self*-love, or *self*-interest. It is never anything as *concrete* as beer, applause, money, or even pleasurable sensations. It must be something relatively *abstract*: one's self, one's welfare, or one's interest. Of course narcissists in the clinical sense do love themselves (their own bodies, really) in a quite literal sense that allows the object of narcissistic desire to be fairly concrete. But psychological egoism is not the view that all motivation is based on narcissistic sexual desires. The self that the psychological egoist says we love is not so concrete. For that reason, the view of the extreme psychological egoist is rather mysterious. The ultimate motivation which that view attributes to us has an object which is not all that easy to specify.

These two observations lead naturally to Butler's basic objection to extreme psychological egoism. Of course, he says, there are more desires in the 'soul' than the extreme version allows. There are also all sorts of individual desires for particular objects, some of them fairly concrete. For example, if I am hungry, I have a desire *for some food* now. Only when some disease makes me incapable of appetite, but I feel I should eat anyway to keep up my strength, do I desire food *only* as a means to self-interest. More usually I desire the food itself, as well as the good it does me. Again, I might desire applause, or fame, or sexual pleasure, or respect, etc.; and even if I sometimes desire these things as a means to other things, I usually desire them also for themselves as well. Butler calls desires such as these 'appetites'. Butler wants to argue two things against the extreme psychological egoist. First, the objects of these common appetites are not desired merely as a means to some relatively abstract object of desire called 'the self' or 'self-interest'. We do in fact have appetites for other particular things, where we desire these objects not just (if at all) as means, but for themselves. Second, the very notion of self-interest (self-love) presupposes, and is constructed out of, particular appetites for particular objects. Hence Butler calls them 'primary appetites'. They are primary in the sense that 'secondary' motivations such as self-interest must presuppose their existence. Butler has three arguments for the existence and primacy of primary appetites.

(1) The content argument

It seems quite impossible to give any content to self-interest (to determine what is in one's self-interest) without supposing one to have particular appetites for particular things. It's hard to imagine a being with absolutely no primary appetites (a totally indifferent being without even a desire to live or die) still having a concept of self-interest. Without the primary appetites, self-love would seem to have nothing to work on. This brings us to the second argument.

53

(2) The reflective nature of self-love

What we call self-interest takes a long-term view. It typically reflects on the conflicts between one's own various primary appetites (including, notably, those we don't have at present but will have) and attempts to 'adjudicate' the conflicts. It's self-love that tells you (whether or not you comply) that having a fifth piece of gâteau is less important than not feeling sick later, or that taking out a certain kind of insurance is more important than spending the money on some present object, or that it would be prudent to control your temper in a dangerous situation. But self-love can adjudicate in this way only if there are primary appetites capable of coming into conflict (e.g. desire for cake and aversion to getting sick).

The arguments in (1) and (2) now explain why it is wrong to think of the object of self-love (self-interest) as being some distinct object, the 'self' or 'one's welfare', toward which we have a strange fixation or yen. This misunderstands self-love. It is not a passion for some strangely abstract object. Rather, it is a secondary motivation operating upon, as its content, the various primary appetites one has, taking a long-term, reflective view and adjudicating the conflicts that arise at the primary level. It is not a further, separate passion or appetite, so much as a way of organizing the appetites one already has.

(3) Weakness of will

That self-love and the various primary appetites are distinct principles of motivation seems particularly clear from the fact that they can actually come into conflict. Not only may primary appetites conflict with other primary appetites, primary appetites sometimes conflict with self-love itself. Thus even when I know self-love requires that I forgo that further piece of gâteau, I can all too easily give in to my primary appetite for cake, even knowingly acting against my own self-interest. This is a kind of 'weakness of will' (here not moral weakness but prudential weakness of will). There are two points to be made here. First, that there is a motivational conflict at all in cases of weakness of the will shows that there is more than self-love about as a motivation. What can conflict with self-love (rather than just serve it, as 'reason' does) must be another principle of motivation. Second, the primary appetites are not only capable of conflicting with self-love, they can sometimes even win out over self-love. Self-love is occasionally not even the strongest motivation about. Butler is rather fond of making the point that, so far from being solely motivated by self-love, we are, sadly, too often insufficiently motivated by self-love. Butler would like to see a bit more self-love around.

Argument (3) is a matter of saying, to the psychological egoist, that if he concedes there is such a thing as weakness of will, he must concede there are primary appetites for self-love to conflict with. Arguments (1) and (2) are a matter of saying that if he concedes there is such a thing as self-love at all, he must further concede there are primary appetites for it to operate on. If one lets in self-love at all into one's psychological theory, one cannot keep out the horde of primary appetites as well. Hence *extreme* psychological egoism is not a possible position. If self-love is one motivation, it cannot be the only motivation.

The psychological egoist will probably not feel dismayed at all by Butler's arguments against the extreme position. Indeed the psychological egoist may well feel Butler's argument is working into his hands. After all, appetites for food, sex, fame, etc. don't look like much of a shift away from egoism. The only lesson to be learned from Butler might seem to be that it would be silly to suppose that rational self-interest or prudence could be the only motivations we have. But why suppose rational self-interest is the only selfish motive? My digging into another piece of gâteau still looks rather selfish, even if perhaps not all that prudent. So the moral of the *first stage* of Butler's argument seems to be a very modest one, i.e. that we shouldn't be *extreme* psychological egoists. A psychological egoist might regard that as merely a very good reason for being a *moderate* psychological egoist.

Stage 2: The refutation of moderate psychological egoism

The *moderate psychological egoist* adjusts his thesis in the minimal way necessary to avoid the objection in stage 1. He holds that human motivation consists of: (1) primary appetites, just as Butler says; (2) self-love, as a motivation secondary to, and reflective upon, primary appetites, but still capable of coming into conflict with them; and (3) 'reason', not an independent principle of motivation but only a tool of self-love. It appears the moderate psychological egoist simply takes advantage of all of Butler's hard work. However, letting in the primary appetites is something like letting in the Trojan horse. Admitting the primary appetites makes possible Butler's next argument.

Primary appetites have something like the form 'I now desire . . . ', or 'I have an aversion to . . . '. Now it is of course a matter for empirical investigation what things I do have a desire, or else aversion, for, and which things I have no desires in regard to. Given human nature, there are, no doubt, many empirical limitations on what sorts of things I can desire, but there don't seem to be a great many *logical* (or *conceptual*) limits to what might be the object of a possible desire or aversion. At least objects such as those in the following two groups do not seem to be ruled out simply on logical grounds as possible objects of desire:

(a) to eat a piece of gâteau, to receive an ovation, to have a glass of beer now, etc. (all for oneself);
(b) that a child smile, that a certain other person do well, that a certain suffering in another be alleviated, etc. (all in regard to others).

Butler calls appetites for objects like those in (a) 'self-regarding' appetites, and appetites for objects such as we find in (b) 'other-regarding' appetites. In both cases the primary appetites in question are for these objects themselves, not just for those objects as means. (For example, it's not just that one wants the child to smile so one can take a prize-winning photograph.)

Butler claims that the ordinary, and useful, distinction we mark with the terms 'selfish desires' and 'unselfish desires' is a matter of the kind of object of the desire. Roughly, selfish desires are for 'self-regarding' objects such as those in (a). On the other hand, desires for 'other-regarding' objects such as those in (b) would get classified as unselfish. Of course Butler is not saying that all primary appetites can be classified as either self-regarding or other-regarding. Some kinds of primary appetites may be somewhat borderline, not clearly classifiable in either the one class or the other. Furthermore, some other primary appetites may be such as clearly to fall in neither group but to belong in some third category, such as the desires:

   (c) that a certain other person fail miserably, that he suffer, etc.

We might call these 'purely malicious' primary appetites. They seem to be neither egoistic nor altruistic. The same might be said of spite and revenge. However, Butler doesn't have to argue that the self-regarding/other-regarding distinction is exhaustive, or without any overlap, or without borderline cases. All he has to show is that there are at least some clear cases of objects which would count as 'other-regarding' objects, and that one cannot, just from the armchair on a priori grounds, rule out such objects as possible objects of desire. How can the psychological egoist claim to know, before he goes out and does some empirical investigating, that no appetites are for objects such as we find in (b)? If primary appetites are possible, why couldn't almost anything be a logically possible object of appetite? At any rate, why suppose the things in (b) (or for that matter (c)) cannot be desired for themselves?

   In short, Butler claims three things: (1) that there seem to be few logical limits on what might be the object of a primary appetite; more specifically, (2) that other-regarding objects are not to be ruled out as logically possible objects of appetites; and (3) that the ordinary distinction in English between selfish and unselfish is a matter of the kind of object of the desire – roughly selfish desires are for 'self-regarding' objects and unselfish desires are for 'other-regarding' objects. From (1), (2), and (3) Butler concludes (4) that we cannot exclude on purely logical or conceptual grounds the possibility of unselfish desires (not to mention non-selfish ones such as malice and spite). Psychological egoism isn't something knowable a priori in the philosophical armchair.

Owners and objects of desire

Butler's discussion shows that the following is a fallacious argument:

   (i) I am motivated by *my* appetite (desire) for object O.

Therefore

   (ii) The appetite (desire) for O which motivates me is a *selfish* motivation.

Butler's point about the ordinary use of 'selfish' is that it marks a (useful) distinction in terms of kinds of *objects* of desires, and not a (useless) distinction in terms of the *ownership* of the desire. To recommend that we from now on make ownership of the desire rather than the kind of object desired the criterion of a 'selfish' desire is just to recommend that we ruin what has been hitherto a very useful term. 'Selfish' marks a useful contrast where it marks a contrast between desires for certain kinds of objects as opposed to desires for other kinds of objects. But 'selfish' will mark no useful contrast if all that makes a desire 'selfish' is that it is *one's own* desire (whatever its object). That would serve only to make the phrase 'selfish desire' a redundant expression. There *couldn't* be any other kind that one could have. My 'selfishness' would be nothing more than my being motivated by *my* desires. But who else's desires could I be motivated by? And if I somehow could be motivated by your desire, it would still be *my* being motivated.

Thus Butler's argument refutes those who say 'All primary appetites are selfish' not because they have undertaken any scientific enquiry into the objects of actual human desires but only because they have decided to use the word 'selfish' in a new way to mean nothing more than 'motivated by one's motivations'. If this reform succeeded the result would be nothing more exciting than the rendering redundant of the term 'selfish desire'. A further likely result, however, is the sowing of confusion among those who wrongly thought the word was still being used in the old, useful way.

Butler's philosophical psychology

Butler's argument against psychological egoism leaves him with three kinds of motivations, i.e. two kinds of primary appetites, namely self-regarding and other-regarding, and one second-order, reflective motivation, namely self-love. However, Butler thinks there are more kinds of motivation than this in the human psychology. Butler argues for two further motivational principles. One of these he calls 'benevolence'. (We should by now be less dismissive of his eighteenth-century vocabulary.) If self-love is some kind of long-term, reflective, adjudicative principle operating on one's self-regarding primary appetites, then there would seem to be the possibility of a similar second-order principle of motivation which operates on other-regarding appetites instead. This is benevolence. Indeed it would seem that benevolence, which takes a long-term view of the welfare of others, might well come into conflict with a particular other-regarding appetite. For example, parents sometimes give in to the wide-eyed tears or the cute entreaties of a child while knowing that doing so is actually contrary to the long-term welfare and health of that child. Here a primary other-regarding appetite wins out over benevolence.

The other motivational principle Butler adds to the picture he calls 'conscience'. This term is meant to cover moral motivations. An example might be being motivated by a sense of justice or fair play. Butler thinks this is a possible motivation too. It is not to be confused with self-love. For example, the right kind of person might be motivated (at least a bit) to do an act A just because he has promised to do A. 'Conscience' is also not to be confused with benevolence, although it may seem tempting to do so. Butler says we can imagine a person in a situation where he believes (rightly or wrongly) that either of the two choices open to him is equally benevolent although one involves lying (or punishing the innocent, or breaking a promise) while the other does not. It seems possible a person might be motivated by the moral belief that lying (or punishing the innocent, or breaking a promise) is wrong. Anyone so motivated would have to be motivated by something other than benevolence, because he believes the alternatives to be equally benevolent.

It should be noted that it will be particularly difficult for anyone who has conceded the possibility of self-love as a principle of motivation to deny the possibility of moral motivation. The 'prudential' motivation of self-love seems already to involve something 'normative' about it. Self-love takes a certain long-term view and 'adjudicates' between conflicting primary appetites. Having a sense of self-love seems to involve commitment to a number of normative claims, such as 'My (present) desire for A *should* give way to my (future) desire for B'. Even when, out of weakness of will, one actually gives in to the desire for A, it can be with the concurrent thought that one is making a mistake. As Butler puts it, self-love continues to claim 'authority' even when it lacks the 'power' over the primary appetites. But if something like this is admitted to go on in the case of self-love, it will be difficult to maintain that conscience cannot be a motivation, or anyway to maintain this on the ground that thoughts about what one *should* do can never be a motivation. Self-love already seems to involve, quite centrally, motivating thoughts about what desires *should* give way to what others. If one really thinks conscience is impossible as a motivation, one must rethink whether even self-love can be a motivation. Moral motivation seems no more implausible than prudential motivation.

The slide into psychological egoism

Consider these four propositions in sequence:

(1) Persons are motivated only by their motivations.

Hence

(2) Persons are motivated only by their (primary) desires or wants.

Hence

(3) Persons are motivated only by selfish desires and wants.

Hence

(4) No one ever intentionally acts contrary to what he believes is to his greatest self-interest.

An easy way to slide into psychological egoism (via confusion rather than with reason) is to suppose that each proposition entails, or just is, the proposition below it. However, at each of the three transitions in this slide, Butler has an important objection to make. The move from (1) to (2) has the effect of eliminating conscience as well as self-love and benevolence as possible motivations. But there must be better reasons produced for believing these are not possible motivations than just one's inability to distinguish the meaning of (2) from the meaning of (1). The slide from (2) to (3) involves the outright confusion between the ownership of a desire and the desire's having a self-regarding object. And while (3) rather than (4) is psychological egoism, some are tempted to slide from (3) to (4) as well. To do so ignores the possibility of (prudential) weakness of will and various other kinds of breakdowns and irrationality in carrying out actions. Proposition (4) cannot possibly be right. Yet sometimes (2), (3), and even (4) are treated as mere truisms by those who do not properly distinguish them from (1), which of course is a truism. (Who else's motivations could one be motivated by?) If there is an argument for psychological egoism, it should be based on actual evidence and reputable scientific theorizing. It should not just be a matter of sliding down the egoist's slide. Certainly it should be more than proposing to use the word 'selfish' in a new and particularly useless way. Butler's argument tosses the psychological egoist out of his smug reclining position in the philosophical armchair and hands him the spade to do some actual empirical enquiry.

PSYCHOLOGICAL HEDONISM

One of the basic moves in Butler's refutation of psychological egoism applies equally to psychological hedonism. One wonders why the object of a primary appetite couldn't (logically) be almost anything. Why must (*logically* 'must') it be only for pleasure sensations (and to avoid pain sensations)? While this might happen to turn out to be a fact about human desires, one would not really expect to be able to know this in the philosophical armchair, before actually going out and investigating what sorts of objects human desires had. However, this Butler objection, while it may loosen things up a bit, is rarely very persuasive to those who feel that pleasure and the avoidance of pain just *have to be* the only ultimate motivations, that one *couldn't* conceivably desire anything else (except as a means).

I think this is because there are more confusions behind psychological hedonism (behind these 'have to be' and 'just couldn't' feelings) than the ones Butler notes in regard to psychological egoism. Psychological hedonism has its own specialized confusions as well. Some of these are to be found in what we might call the 'hedonist's slide':

(1) A person wants something (or at least acts on that want) only if he thinks there is a (real) chance of the desire's being *satisfied*.

Hence

(2) A person wants something only if he thinks he is going to *get some satisfaction* from getting what he wants.

Hence

(3) A person wants something only *for the pleasure* of getting what he wants.

61

Hence

(4) A person wants only *pleasure sensations* (as ends); everything else that is desired is desired only as a means to pleasure sensations.

One of the things that makes the hedonist's slide illegitimate is that there seem to be several importantly different senses of 'satisfaction' (and also of 'pleasure') about. Under certain senses of 'satisfaction' the propositions toward the top of the slide come close to being true (although they are perhaps not quite truisms). The illegitimacy comes in substituting other senses of 'satisfaction' to get the propositions further down. The slide consists in not noticing one has done this, in thinking one still has the relatively innocuous proposition one began with at the top. One bit of linguistic evidence that might make us suspect that there are several senses of 'satisfaction' is that there seem to be, not one, but several 'opposites' to 'satisfaction', e.g. 'frustration', 'dissatisfaction', 'boredom', 'pain'. While it is only a beginning, we might distinguish four importantly different senses of 'satisfaction' and/or 'pleasure' in ordinary usage:

(a) A somewhat archaic sense

A now fairly unusual sense of 'being satisfied' is just 'getting the thing which you desired'. It's a bit analogous to the way in which mathematicians speak of the values which 'satisfy' an equation. I'm not sure we ever use the word 'satisfaction' purely in this sense. But it's worth discussing because, of all the senses, it is the one that comes closest to making (1) in the hedonist's slide true. So interpreted, (1) says that we don't want (or at least don't try to get) what we know we have no chance of getting. Even so, this is only 'close to true'. Those hopelessly in love sometimes continue to want what they know they will never get, and those people who act against all hope actually take steps that they know will be in vain. Whether or not this is rational, it clearly does occur. But, apart from such cases, (1) seems to be generally true for 'satisfaction' as interpreted in the archaic sense.

(b) The non-disappointment sense

The archaic sense cannot be that in which we usually use the word. We sometimes ask people, after they get what they wanted, 'Well, are you satisfied now?' This question would not make sense if 'satisfied' were used in the archaic sense. It would be like asking 'Now that you've got what you wanted, have you got what you wanted?' Instead, the question seems to be asking whether one is disappointed now, whether one has changed one's mind now that one sees what it's like, whether one regrets getting what one formerly wanted. So it seems that there is another sense of 'satisfaction', which just adds a further condition onto the meaning of the archaic sense, (a). Under this second sense, (b), 'satisfaction' means 'getting what you wanted and then not regretting it or being disappointed'. This sense of 'satisfaction' might, when substituted in proposition (1) of the hedonist's slide, make that proposition approach truth. Certainly it seems *irrational* to act on a desire while knowing that one will regret it or be disappointed when one gets the thing desired. However, I'm not sure that we aren't, none the less, sometimes irrational in just that way. We may act on desires for things that we know will only be ashes in the mouth on first taste. But apart from such cases, this sense of 'satisfaction' might make (1) come close to the truth.

The desire for 'satisfaction' in this second sense, (b), must be construed as a second-order desire. It is the (second-order) desire that when one gets what one (first-order) desires one will not be disappointed. This is important for several reasons. First, the second-order desire for 'satisfaction' in this sense could not be the only sort of desire we have, for one's having second-order desires presupposes that there are other first-order desires for them to be about. Second, *what* is desired at the first-order level is left entirely open as regards this definition of 'satisfaction'. There was no assumption that it always has to be for something like pleasure sensations. Finally, it seems quite upside down to suppose that in such cases the things desired at the first-order level are only desired as a means to what is desired at the second-order level. Rather, it would seem one just desires the things (whatever they are) at the first-order level, but also has some additional, second-order desires regarding certain first-order desires. In all of this there is nothing like a commitment to psychological hedonism. This sense of 'satisfaction' leaves it entirely open

63

what sorts of things we desire at the first-order level. Of course the use of the word 'satisfaction' in propositions like (1) and (2) of the hedonist's slide can superficially look like hedonistic claims even when, as when sense (b) is employed, they are not that at all.

(c) The enjoyment sense

One meaning of the word 'pleasure' is just 'enjoyment'. We have a number of near synonyms to cover this notion, e.g. 'have fun doing activity A', 'get a lot of satisfaction out of doing A', 'take pleasure in doing A', 'do A just for the fun of it', 'do A just for pleasure', and, finally, 'just enjoy doing A'. The psychological hedonist's account of enjoyment will say that the 'pleasure' one takes in the activities one enjoys is invariably a bodily sensation (or a qualitative experiential state) which is causally produced by the activities, and, furthermore, that one only undertakes the activities in order to get these sensations.

The hedonist's account of 'enjoying doing an activity A' is very far from plausible, and has certain well-known difficulties. The main attack on the hedonist's account of enjoyment comes from the Aristotle–Ryle account of enjoyment. The A–R account of enjoyment involves three observations about enjoying:

(i) Enjoyment is always of some activity. There is no such state or activity as just enjoying (full stop). There is something very odd about saying, 'I did *three* things this afternoon, played chess, played tennis, and enjoyed.'

(ii) Enjoyment is 'activity-specific' (see Urmson 1967). The pleasure (i.e. enjoyment) of an activity intensifies that activity but the pleasure (enjoyment) of another activity typically interferes with the doing of the original activity. For example, the pleasure of playing chess intensifies the playing of chess, but the pleasure of listening to the music in the background is apt to interfere with the playing of chess. Here the pleasure of playing chess (as when I say I take pleasure in playing chess) is not to be identified with the occasional momentary feelings of elation I might get on seeing a particularly effective move. (*That* might very well interfere with my chess-playing until I calm down.) I can say I enjoyed playing chess this afternoon even when no such moments of elation occurred. Nor do I in fact play chess to get these occasional spasms of elation (although they are nice, too). If I really enjoy chess, what I like is the activity of playing chess. ('And why couldn't the being engaged in this activity be the object of a desire?' Butler might ask.) That takes us to the third observation.

(iii) To enjoy an activity is certainly not merely to desire it as a means to something else, distinct from the doing of that activity. It is not to desire it only as a means. Someone who engaged in tennis activity only because it causally produced certain sensations which he couldn't get with less running about would not really enjoy tennis at all. He would probably resent having to do all that running about, and would give it up like that if, for example, the right sorts of electrodes implanted in his brain could produce the desired sensations directly.

The Aristotle–Ryle account of enjoyment denies that it is something separate from the doing of the enjoyed activity. Instead it is said to be a way of engaging in the activity. It's not something that happens at the same time, but is rather a matter of how you engage in the activity. For example, it's said to be a matter of being engrossed in the activity, lost in the activity, etc., rather than, say, drumming one's fingers and counting the minutes until it will be over (being bored, as we say). The Aristotle–Ryle account is controversial and probably goes too far in down-playing the role of sensations and qualitative states of experience. But even if we don't go as far as Aristotle and Ryle in their account of enjoyment, we can accept the three observations (i)–(iii) as posing distinct difficulties for the hedonist's causal account.

Language perhaps misleads us into hedonistic confusions. The sentence 'He plays tennis just for the money (or for his health, or to make business contacts)' has the same grammatical form as 'He plays tennis just for fun'. This superficial grammatical similarity might mislead us into thinking that in the latter case, just as in the former, the tennis is desired only as a means to something distinct from it. But in fact the function of phrases like 'just for fun' or 'just for pleasure' is precisely to *deny* that the activity is only undertaken as a means to separate ends. There is something odd about saying a person plays tennis just for the enjoyment of it, but that at the same time he actually hates tennis, and engages in it only as a means to something else which he is really after, namely the enjoyment of it. Thinking that when we enjoy doing an activity we regard the activity only as a means to something else (the 'pleasure') seems to be as bad a mistake as, to use Quine's example, trying to reify 'sakes'. The mistake of reifying 'sakes' is that of supposing that a sentence like 'Jane did it only for John's sake' is to be understood on the analogy of 'Jane did it only for John's money', i.e. that there must be some kind of an entity called a 'sake' which Jane was really after, having no use for John himself at all. We need to avoid the mistake of falling into believing psychological hedonism where we have no good empirical or scientific grounds for believing it, but have only been misled by the grammatical form of certain sentences containing the words 'pleasure' or 'satisfaction'.

(d) The bodily pleasures sense

Certainly the Aristotle–Ryle account plausibly applies only to one use, not to all uses of the word 'pleasure'. Sometimes 'pleasure' is indeed used to refer to pleasure sensations or pleasure feelings. In this sense of 'pleasure' it makes sense to ask when the sensation or feeling occurred, how long it lasted, whether it was more or less intense than some other sensation. Sometimes it makes sense to ask just where the pleasure was felt, in what part of the body. Usually the opposite of a pleasure sensation is thought to be a pain sensation (rather than boredom, dissatisfaction, etc.). Pains and pleasures in this sense are what the hedonist is talking about. It cannot be the other three senses that we have just discussed, for they all leave open the question of what may be the objects of our desires. The hedonist, however, thinks that ultimately all our desires are to have, or to avoid, certain experiences or sensations – things which have intensity, duration, etc. Of course non-hedonists admit that bodily pleasures are among the objects of desire, but do not suppose they are the only things we can desire for themselves.

Distinguishing these four senses of 'pleasure' (and 'satisfaction') puts the psychological hedonist on the defensive. He can no longer rely on simply confusing these senses to make his case seem plausible. The first three senses, (a)–(c), are ordinary usages that do not involve any commitment to psychological hedonism. All three leave it quite open what sorts of things are the objects of desires (when these objects are desired for themselves rather than just as means). The main way in which psychological hedonism is made to seem plausible is by confusing sense (a) or (b) or (c) with the sensation/experience sense, (d). Once we sweep aside that particular series of confusions, the basic Butler point seems to come back into its own. What reason have we to suppose that there are terribly narrow or stringent logical limits on what might be the object of a desire or a want? Just as there is no reason to restrict these objects to self-regarding objects, there is even less reason to restrict them to pleasure and pain avoidance.

ARE PSYCHOLOGICAL EGOISM AND HEDONISM REALLY REFUTED?

While the word has recently been ruined by journalists, strictly speaking the word 'refutation' is a term of success: it means a demonstration of falsehood. Do Butler's arguments succeed against psychological egoism (and a *fortiori* against psychological hedonism)? I think that depends on the kinds of psychological egoism (or hedonism) in question. On one hand, psychological egoism and hedonism could be *conceptual* (or logical) theses, i.e. claims that it is conceptually (logically) impossible for there to be any other kinds of motivations. Those who hold this sort of view are the armchair egoists and hedonists. On the other hand, they could be more modest, *empirical* claims that while other kinds of motivations are logically possible, as a matter of empirical fact only these special kinds of motivations do occur. The arguments we have discussed above can claim to refute the conceptual (logical) versions of psychological egoism and hedonism. Of course it is not always going to be clear whether a particular egoist (or hedonist) is defending the conceptual rather than the empirical version of his thesis. But there are often some clues. For example, suppose we offer a putative empirical counter-example to one of these theses, based on everyday observation, e.g. someone like Albert Schweizer, who seems to have done a great many non-egoistic, non-hedonistic things. If the reply to the purported counter-example is 'Well, all that shows is that Albert got his kicks in peculiar ways', we have reason to suspect we are up against an armchair rather than an empirical psychological egoist. How does he know that this must be so? Well, presumably only because his psychological egoism or hedonism requires it to be so. If, on the other hand, he actually had some evidence in hand, or a theoretical basis of a sort not to beg the question, that would be quite different. For example, if he actually had a secret diary of Albert Schweizer, which put things in a rather different light from that hitherto accepted, that would be reason to think that we had had the good luck to encounter a psychological egoist (or hedonist) willing to defend his thesis on empirical grounds. Let us suppose, then, that psychological egoism (or hedonism) is being put forward, not as a conceptual or logical thesis, but as an empirical, scientific claim. Do Butler's arguments do anything to counter this more moderate version?

At this point Butler's argument has to go a step further. It cannot be content with the claim that non-egoistic (and non-hedonistic) motivations are logically possible; the argument must take the further step of noting that a lot of everyday, common-sense observations seem to support the view that there actually are cases of such motivations. I suspect Butler and others have thought this sort of observation was conclusive, was a 'refutation'. That is putting it a bit too strongly. What such everyday evidence does is shift decisively the burden of proof onto the psychological egoist (and hedonist). They then have the very difficult task of giving good scientific grounds for overturning the prima-facie evidence of everyday common-sense observation. They must provide further evidence and further well-based scientific theorizing to show that common sense has been deceived, not just in a few cases, but on a systematic, global basis. It is of course (logically) *possible* that when we think we are altruistic we are only rationalizing or engaging in self-deception. (But it is also logically possible that when a person represents his act as a hard-headed egoistic one he is really only rationalizing, ashamed of his soft-headed altruism.) But citing mere logical possibilities is not enough. The psychological egoist (or hedonist) must give us some empirically based grounds for thinking that this rationalizing and self-deception actually goes on. Furthermore, he has to show, not just that such self-deception or rationalization does occur sometimes, or even often, he must show it occurs without exception. All of this would not be easy to show.

In summary, the versions of psychological egoism (and hedonism) which are put forward as logical (armchair) theses do seem to have been refuted by Butler-type arguments. On the other hand, the versions which are put forward as empirical theses have a different problem, viz. explaining a lot of everyday common-sense observations to the contrary. After Butler's arguments the discussion was far from over, but things could never be quite the same again. The tables had been turned. Psychological egoists and hedonists have been on the defensive ever since.

FURTHER READING

The primary source for Butler's refutation of psychological egoism is Butler (1726: esp. Sermon xi). For general discussions of psychological egoism, see Brandt (1976), Broad (1949–50), Duncan-Jones (1962: ch. 4), Feinberg (1975: 'Psychological egoism'; also 557–8 for further references), Hobbes (1651), Nagel (1970), and Slote (1964).

For the Aristotle–Ryle account of enjoyment, the primary sources are Aristotle's *Nicomachean Ethics* and Ryle (1949: ch. 4; 1954; 1964: ch. 4). A good survey of views on psychological hedonism is Alston's article 'Pleasure' in Edwards (1967: 341–7). Further useful material may be found in Anscombe (1967), Brandt (1959: ch. 12; 1979: ch. 2; see also 36, n.5 for further references), Gosling (1969), Penelhum (1957), and Urmson (1967).

5

Meta-ethical theories

Chapter 2 discussed authoritarian ethics and subjectivist ethics. Chapter 3 went on to discuss certain important ethical theories which are neither authoritarian nor subjectivist. However, all the theories in both chapters take normative ethics to be formulable in one or more rules or principles. In chapter 10 we will discuss an ethical theory, 'situationalism', which denies that this is possible. We will also discuss in that chapter various ethical theories which make morality relative in various ways, e.g. 'ethical relativism'. However, we have had enough examples of normative ethical theories already to have some idea what a normative ethical theory is like. But what is a meta-ethical theory like? This chapter will discuss the three main types: naturalistic, non-naturalistic, and non-cognitivist.

MORAL VALUES AND NATURALISTIC FACTS

One way of understanding the world is 'naturalistically'. Metaphysical naturalism, as a general philosophical approach, looks to science (or at least the more successful sciences) and the scientific method in order to describe and explain what there is. Typically this will involve thinking in causal terms, describing events in terms of those properties which occur in causal laws. Again, it is typical of a 'naturalistic' description that the properties it mentions are empirical (i.e. in principle detectable by sense experience) or at least are those mentioned in a total theory which is testable or empirical in some sense.

At their present stage of development, the sciences (especially the more successful ones such as chemistry or physics) seem to be 'value-free'. We must be very careful, however, about what we mean by 'value-free' in this context. There are a number of important senses in which the sciences are *not* value-free:

(1) The results and discoveries of the sciences are often of great interest to us when added to the moral values we already have.
(2) The practices and modes of enquiry of science, and its discoveries, are sometimes subject to moral criticisms, given the moral values we already have.
(3) Some sciences study the moral beliefs and values of individuals and cultures.

The sense in which the sciences might arguably be value-free is this:

(4) The claims made in the various reputable sciences make no moral value claims, presuppose no moral value claims, entail no moral value claims.

(Possibly even the purest sciences are not free, in this last sense, of *all* kinds of values. They all seem to presuppose certain claims about what it is *reasonable* to believe, i.e. *ought* to be believed, in the face of certain evidence or premises. But our concern in this chapter is with *moral* value claims. Also, because of their close connection with moral claims, we shall include value claims of type 3 (in chapter 3), judgements of human well-being.)

Metaphysical naturalism holds that everything is to be understood naturalistically. A total, final science would be the whole story about the universe. There are no truths about the universe other than naturalistic ones.

However, if (a) the sciences involve no value claims (at least none of the kind of interest in moral philosophy), and if, furthermore, (b) naturalistic science delivers *all* the truths that there are, then (c) there are no moral truths or moral facts in the world. Now in defence of claim (a), some philosophers have alleged that there is some sort of logical 'gap' between (naturalistic) facts and (moral) values. Indeed there are several, slightly different, sorts of 'gaps' which have been alleged:

(i) No moral judgement just *is* a naturalistic factual claim.
(ii) No moral judgement can be validly *deduced* from a set of premises all of which are naturalistic factual claims.
(iii) No moral, or related value, term (property) can be *defined*

(*analysed*) in terms of naturalistic terms (properties). (The 'naturalistic fallacy' thesis.)

To be sure, none of (i)–(iii) rule out altogether the possibility of moral facts or moral properties. But in that case they would have to be rather queer facts and properties, existing in an autonomous realm logically independent of the naturalistic world, quite unrelated to it by any relation of identity, deduction, or definition.

META-ETHICAL NATURALISM

Meta-ethical naturalists (or just 'naturalists', in this section) deny that there is any deep problem about 'the place of moral values in the world of naturalistic facts'. They simply deny there are any 'gaps' of the sort which lead to such a problem. Specifically, they deny (iii) above (and, as a consequence, deny (i) and (ii) as well). They claim that moral terms are definable in terms of naturalistic terms or that moral properties just *are* naturalistic ones. Thus we do not need to suppose that moral properties belong to some strange, autonomous, non-naturalistic realm. Actually they turn out to be ordinary, naturalistic properties which could just as well be picked out by expressions without the moral flavour of the traditional ethical vocabulary.

Let us consider some examples. The late nineteenth-century theory (sometimes called 'evolutionary ethics') propagated by Herbert Spencer is represented by G.E. Moore (1903: ch. 2) as being an instance of meta-ethical naturalism. Evolutionary meta-ethics holds:

D1 'Good' *just means* 'evolutionarily (relatively) advanced'.

or perhaps that:

D1′ The property of being good just *is* the property of being evolutionarily (relatively) advanced.

The notion of being evolutionarily advanced is supposedly a naturalistic one, its sense being provided by its (supposed) role in the classical theory of evolution.

Evolutionary meta-ethics is untypical in one respect. It is more usual for meta-ethical naturalists to bring psychological (especially motivational) notions into their definitions. For example, some other alleged naturalistic definitions are:

D2 'Good' means 'pleasant'.

D3 'Good' means 'what one desires (perhaps at a deeper level of consciousness) to desire'.

D4 'Wrong' means 'what I tend to feel moral disapproval toward'.

The anthropologist Westermarck, the philosopher R.B. Perry, and the psychologist B.F. Skinner appear to have given motivationally laden naturalistic definitions of various value terms.

One influential naturalist view is that of Thomas Aquinas, who gives something like the following definition of (non-moral, presumably) good, a definition which contains a conspicuous motivational element:

D5 'Good' means 'that which all things (naturally, or by their nature) seek after'.

(Aquinas then gives a teleological account of moral rightness, as doing or pursuing what is good.) Of course, to know what things *are good* for humans, as opposed to what goodness *is*, requires a further, substantive study of human nature and its strivings.

Moore's attack on naturalism

G.E. Moore (1903) employed his famous 'open question' argument against naturalistic definitions like those listed above. He noted that we can *sensibly* raise questions such as:

Q1 Are evolutionarily more advanced societies always better?

Q2 Are pleasant things invariably good?

Q3 Are all of our natural inclinations toward good things only?

Now these seem like *real issues*, i.e. open questions. This is so even if in the end affirmative answers are to be given to these questions. They are still real questions, worth asking. But if, for example, 'good' just meant 'pleasant' it would be a silly question to ask 'Are pleasant things invariably good?', as silly as asking 'Are vixens invariably female?' or 'Do you suppose any bachelors are married?' Such questions appear to demonstrate, by the mere asking, an ignorance of the language or of the concepts employed.

The argument against supposing that 'good' means 'pleasant' might be put as follows. If 'good' meant 'pleasant', then asking 'Are pleasant things always good?' would be silly. But, whatever the actual answer, the question 'Are pleasant things always good?'

is not silly – it marks some real issue, it is an 'open' question. Thus the proposed naturalistic definition must be mistaken.

Now Moore thought that he could use the open question argument to defeat not only the above particular naturalistic definition, but *any* naturalistic definition. Whenever a naturalist attempts to define any ethical term, 'E', in terms of a naturalistic term 'N', Moore will insist that there is an appropriate question of the form 'Are things having N always E?' Moore thinks we will always see that this is an *open* question. But the question could not mark a real issue if the proposed naturalistic definition of 'E' were correct. So it must be incorrect. Thus the mistake is not one just a few naturalists make. *Any* naturalistic definition of *any* ethical or value term must be mistaken. Hence Moore called it, not just a mistake, but a 'fallacy', the 'naturalistic fallacy'.

Supernatural and theistic meta-ethics

The *super*naturalist fares no better than the naturalist in the face of Moore's attack. It is always a mistake to define an evaluative term purely in terms of non-evaluative notions (whether natural or supernatural). For example, suppose a theist alleged:

D6 'Morally right' just means 'commanded by God'.

Moore would allege it is a real question whether one ought to do what God commands. Surely it seems a real question as to whether Abraham should have obeyed God's command to sacrifice Isaac. (It is *still* a real question if the answer turns out to be 'Yes'!) Furthermore, if the above definition were correct, saying that it is right to obey God would be as empty as saying 'What God commands is what God commands'. (That's no more interesting than saying 'What Hitler commands is what Hitler commands'!) Frankena (1930) renamed Moore's 'naturalistic fallacy' the 'definist fallacy', just because it appears to hold against *any* attempt, naturalistic or supernaturalistic, to define value terms solely in terms of non-evaluative terms.

Moore's non-naturalism

Moore's argument allows that some moral terms may have definitions, as long as these definitions involve at least some other moral terms. (For example, moral *goodness* in persons might be some disposition to do acts because they are morally *right*.) However, to avoid circularity we must eventually get to some terms which are not further definable in moral terms. (Moore thought 'good' was such a primitive, i.e. logically prior, notion.) Given that such a value term can be given no naturalistic (or supernaturalistic) definition, it must then be a primitive (i.e. unanalysable), non-natural property. If this sounds mysterious, remember that many *natural* properties are primitive (i.e. unanalysable). The property of *yellow* seems to be one.

One might feel driven to Moore's non-naturalism once one sees that all forms of naturalism have been ruled out by Moore's open question argument. But it is not a view which is very plausible in its own right. It has several serious difficulties to overcome:

1 *The epistemological problem* If goodness is a non-natural property, how do we detect it in things? Certainly not by the usual senses, for that would make it naturalistic. The only answer which suggests itself (one which did not attract Moore) is that we have a special faculty, a 'moral sense', for detecting good and bad or right and wrong. However, such a supposition faces serious difficulties. If perceiving good were something like perceiving yellow, we would expect a high degree of agreement among perceivers. Instead, we find a great deal of disagreement about moral matters. Admittedly, people do sometimes misperceive yellow; perhaps we should consider the possibility that moral disagreement is due, similarly, to malfunctions of the alleged 'moral sense'. But then how could we decide, non-arbitrarily, whose 'moral sense' was malfunctioning? In the case of colour-blindness, or other such malfunctions, we have some idea what organs and mechanisms are involved and what has gone wrong, but no such organ or area in the brain has been identified as the 'goodness detector'.

2 *The motivational problem* Believing that something is good (or, perhaps, that something is right) seems to involve more than just *detecting* a property in a thing, a property to which one might be indifferent. It appears, *of necessity*, to involve some (even if only slight) disposition to act and feel in certain ways in regard to that thing. This view is sometimes called 'internalism', i.e. the view that to assent (sincerely) to a moral or value judgement *necessarily* involves some tendency to act and/or feel in certain ways. But if good (or wrong) are simply properties of things (even if non-naturalistic ones) it's hard to see why internalism should

be true. What would be *impossible* about 'detecting' a thing's goodness but being totally indifferent (at every level of conscious-ness) to it: 'More goodness here. . . . Boring!'? If Moore's view is right, why should goodness have a more intimate connection with choice or action than yellowness does?

3 *The role of reasons* The moral and value judgements we make are often based on *reasons* which mention natural properties (e.g. 'This act is wrong because it would *harm* others, or right because it is what one *promised*'). Moore's view needs to explain how the presence of natural properties could ever be a *reason* for the presence of non-natural properties. (Moore claimed that non-natural properties 'supervened' on natural properties. But this notion requires further explanation.)

In summary, Moore's open question argument would seem to have disposed of all naturalistic meta-ethical theories as well as all super-naturalistic ones. However, his own non-naturalism is quite implausible for the reasons just mentioned. But if both naturalism and non-naturalism are to be rejected, where does that leave us?

NON-COGNITIVISM

If naturalism and non-naturalism are to be rejected, the alternative is to deny the assumption accepted by both the naturalist and the non-naturalist, i.e. that moral terms ascribe properties to things. Thus moral judgements are perhaps not to be seen as true (or even false!) allegations of fact. They are neither statements of naturalistic fact nor statements of non-naturalistic fact.

Moore claimed there was a certain 'gap' between moral judge-ments (and properties) and naturalistic ones. But perhaps the gap runs much deeper. The gap may divide the moral from all of the *factual* (whether natural or non-natural). Thus we may envisage these three gaps:

(i') *Non-cognitivism*: No moral judgement just *is* a (true or false) statement of fact.

(ii') *Hume's gap*: No moral judgement can be logically *deduced* from a set of premises consisting only of (true or false) statements of fact.

(iii') No moral predicate simply ascribes (truly or falsely) *a property* to something.

A non-cognitivist is anyone who holds (i'). Furthermore, if one holds (i'), one *must* (on certain plausible assumptions in logic) hold (ii') and (iii') as well.

In this century there are two main reasons why some philosophers have been led to espouse non-cognitivism. The apparent failure of both naturalism and non-naturalism suggests, as we have seen, that the only remaining alternative, non-cognitivism, must be right. But many twentieth-century *empiricist* philosophers have embraced non-cognitivism about moral judgements because they thought it followed from certain theses they held about language in general.

These philosophers claimed that there are just two ways of using language which is 'cognitively meaningful', i.e. a matter of making true, or false, claims. First, a sentence might be used to make an *analytic* claim, i.e. one which is true or false just in virtue of the meaning of the terms involved. Second, a sentence might be used to make a (true or false) *empirical* claim. Empiricists, like A.J. Ayer (1936), typically held that to be empirical a claim must be in principle verifiable (or falsifiable) by sense observations.

Where does this leave moral judgements? Of course there are some analytic propositions which refer to moral notions, e.g. 'A is wrong if A is not permissible'. But such claims do not seem to be moral judgements. (They certainly don't tell us what to do or how to assess.) Empiricists tend to regard such claims (and meta-ethics in general) as merely claims about concepts or the meanings of terms. Thus, analytic claims involving moral concepts, while cognitive, do not make moral judgements.

But if substantive moral judgements are not analytic, neither do they seem to be simply empirical. It is hardly clear what sense experience would verify or falsify any moral judgement, in such a way as to completely account for its meaning. Thus, many empiricists reason, moral judgements, being neither analytic nor empirical, are not cognitive at all. While moral language has some sort of meaningfulness, it is not just cognitive meaningfulness. So many empiricists tend to embrace non-cognitivism in meta-ethics as a consequence of their empiricism.

Now a non-cognitivist (whether or not he bases it on empiricism) still has to give some account of what moral judgements *are*, given that he thinks they are *not* statements of fact. Clearly moral judgements play an important part in our daily lives. We are not just clearing our throats or uttering Lewis Carroll-type nonsense. That is not sufficient to show that they have *cognitive* meaning, since we know that (quite apart from moral discourse) a lot of useful everyday language isn't used for stating facts, e.g. interjections ('Ouch!') and commands or requests ('Close the door, please'). But clearly moral discourse has *some* sort of meaning. So if this meaning is not cognitive meaning (i.e. fact-stating meaning), what sort of meaning is it?

Emotivism

One non-cognitivist theory is emotivism. Ayer and Stevenson suggest that moral judgements have a meaning something like interjections. Typically moral judgements have two main functions:

(a) They *express* our moral feelings and attitudes. (Compare how 'Ouch' is used to express pain.)

(b) They are used to *exhort* others into acting or feeling in certain ways. (Compare 'Come on!' shouted at a game.)

Moral judgements are a bit like cheers: 'Hurrah for keeping one's promise!', 'Bah on stealing!' Notice that emotivist meta-ethics departs in an interesting manner from all the cognitivist views we considered in the previous chapter. The emotivist analysis of ethical terms is not a matter of explicit definition. The emotivist does not think the analysis of 'good' will be a matter of saying something of the form ' "good" $=_{df}$ "XYZ" '. Emotivists do not *define* 'good'. Instead they *characterize* its use or function (as being to express and exhort).

Now emotivism can be easily confused with *certain* versions of *subjectivist* naturalism. (The relevant meaning of 'subjectivist' will be discussed in chapter 8.) The difference is a subtle one, indeed one which will provide some test of your philosophical abilities.

One version of subjectivist naturalism holds that moral judgements are *statements about* one's own feelings and attitudes. For example, on this view, 'Murder is wrong' *just means* 'I disapprove of murder'. Or, 'You ought to support your parents' means 'I approve of your supporting your parents'. Such a view is naturalistic because it turns moral claims into factual *descriptions* of states of mind. Morality falls under the science of psychology. By contrast the emotivist does not think moral judgements are statements of fact at all, not even statements of psychological fact. The emotivist says that moral judgements *express* feelings and attitudes, but without stating that one has these feelings or attitudes. By contrast the above version of subjectivist naturalism says that moral judgements *state the fact* that one has these feelings and attitudes. The difference is analogous to the difference between yelling 'Ouch!' when you hit your fingers and reporting 'That hurts' (perhaps to your physician's probings).

Now the distinction between emotivism and this version of subjectivist naturalism may seem like an overly subtle, 'philosophical' one. But Ayer and Stevenson thought it was crucial to distinguish their view, emotivism, from all versions of subjectivist naturalism. The latter, they thought, were subject to some rather devastating objections from which emotivism could escape unscathed (see Moore 1912; Stevenson 1942):

1 In so far as subjectivist naturalism is a version of naturalism, it is subject to the (alleged) open question refutation. It seems to make perfect sense to say 'It's a fact *about me* that I disapprove of abortion, although that fact is compatible with abortion's not being wrong'. But if the above subjectivist naturalist view were correct this statement would mean 'Abortion is wrong, although that is compatible with abortion's not being wrong'. But the latter cannot be the right translation of the former, for while the former is a perfectly reasonable thing to say, the latter is absurd.

2 If 'Abortion is wrong' meant only 'I disapprove of abortion', appropriate responses might be 'Oh, do you?', 'Tell us more about yourself', 'When did you first get these feelings?', or 'All you ever do is talk about yourself'.

3 If 'Abortion is wrong' means 'I disapprove of abortion', then these two expressions should be interchangeable in any context in which either occurs. But 'If abortion is wrong, the behaviour of some doctors is immoral' does not mean the same as 'If I disapprove of abortion, the behaviour of some doctors is immoral'. The former is a not very controversial inference. The latter is a very idiosyncratic moral view.

Criticisms of emotivism

While emotivism avoids the problems of subjectivist naturalism, it nevertheless has some of its own. The following are problems that any sophisticated versions of emotivism will have to work hard to overcome:

1 The emotivist is really giving a revisionary account of moral

disagreement. 'Disagreement' for him is not really disagreement, but only difference in taste. But this doesn't seem to fit everyday experience. We seem genuinely to disagree about moral questions, and sometimes such disagreements get resolved. We change our minds in response to reasoning.

2 We noted that G.E. Moore had a problem about the reasons we give for our moral judgement, which reasons are claims of naturalistic fact. But emotivism also has a problem in this regard. Suppose I tell you that something is wrong and you ask me for a reason why it is wrong and I say something like 'It would harm so-and-so', or 'It would break a promise'. From the emotivist point of view this must all be a bit puzzling. A mere expression of taste would seem to require no evidence, justification, or reason. Of course my attitude may have a genetic explanation (e.g. the socialization process). But the *cause* of my attitude is not the kind of thing I normally mention when giving (justifying) reasons for my judgement.

3 Moral judgements figure in valid arguments, e.g. 'Murder is wrong, pulling the trigger now would be murder, so pulling the trigger now would be wrong'. But recall that validity is (usually) defined in terms of truth. So if (as the emotivist, or any non-cognitivist, says) moral judgements are not the sort of things to be true (or false), how can they figure in *valid* arguments? (Perhaps a wider notion of 'validity' is required.)

4 Emotivism entails that when I make a sincere moral judgement I actually have the appropriate feeling or attitude. But I can sometimes have an attitude of approval or encouragement toward things that I would have to say, if asked, are immoral (e.g. some of the violence in *Mad Max*). On the other hand, I might feel disgust at a person's manner, style, or dress without supposing it immoral. Perhaps the emotivist will say that moral judgements express only one's *moral* attitudes (e.g. righteous indignation, sense of fair play), which may sometimes conflict with other sorts of attitudes (e.g. aesthetic tastes). But then he must explain (in a non-circular fashion) what makes an attitude specifically a *moral* attitude. (See Alston 1968.)

The above four problems are problems for the emotivist whatever his arguments may be for emotivism. However, we should also remember that it is not enough for the emotivist to state his view (and challenge us to refute it decisively). He must also give some reasons or argument in favour of believing it at all. Earlier I suggested that emotivists tend to give two arguments:

(1) The arguments *against* all the obvious alternatives, i.e. naturalism and non-naturalism.
(2) The use of some empiricist criterion of 'cognitive meaningfulness' which excludes moral judgements as 'cognitively meaningful'.

In chapter 6 I shall argue, in regard to (1), that the open question argument is not as decisive against naturalism as it might first appear. In regard to (2), it is worth noting that the various empiricist criteria of meaningfulness tend to exclude far too much. Not only do they exclude moral (and aesthetic, and theological, and metaphysical) judgements, but they also tend to exclude rather important scientific and everyday judgements. Ayer's verifiability criterion illustrates this. Very few factual statements are directly verifiable in the way he requires. Generally we verify statements only with the aid of background theories, often very subtle and complex theories. Examples: 'An electron has just annihilated an armstrong ion' (particle physics); 'If Jones had stopped at the sign, the collision would not have occurred' (legal questions).

Obviously a criterion of 'cognitive meaningfulness' as defective as this is of little use in proving that moral judgements are not cognitive (fact-stating). At this point the burden of proof really is on the empiricist to come up with a more defensible criterion of the 'cognitively meaningful'. Then perhaps he can attempt to show that moral judgements are not cognitive (fact-stating). Until then, this basis for emotivism is a bit shaky.

QUESTION TO PONDER

How would the emotivist handle questions 1–7 raised at the end of chapter 1?

FURTHER READING

Basic discussions of the meta-ethical/normative ethics divide include Hancock (1974: chs 1, 2), who is very clear, Brandt (1959: chs 7, 8), Frankena (1970; 1973: ch. 6), Hudson (1970: ch. 3), Kerner (1966: ch. 1), and Nowell-Smith (1954: chs 2, 3). Hare (1952: ch. 5) gives an important defence of the division, while G.

Warnock (1976: chs 1, 2, 6) and, more openly, M. Warnock (1960) evince some doubt as to its importance for moral philosophy.

Aquinas' theological naturalism is best approached at *Summa Theologica*, II, QQ 90–7, 'Treatise on Law'. Cruder naturalistic accounts are Perry (1954), Skinner (1971), and Westermarck (1932). Field (1921), and more especially Brandt (1979), offer more sophisticated and difficult accounts. Moore (1912) argues against subjective naturalism, and Stevenson (1967) gives a reply. Monro (1967) and Campbell (1981) are useful in clarifying what might be meant by the 'naturalistic fallacy'.

Price (1897) and Reid (1764) are historical percursors of non-naturalist intuitionism as found in Moore (1903: chs 1, 2), and, more persuasively, in Ross (1939: chs 2, 4, 11).

Urmson (1968) is a good history of emotivism. Hume (1739) is an important historical source. Vigorous non-cognitivisms are espoused in Hare (1952), Ayer (1936: ch. 6; 1959), while Stevenson (1945) does most to develop the idea of 'emotive meaning'. Alston (1968) contains a good critical discussion of key issues.

6

Hume's gap and the naturalistic fallacy

In chapter 5 I discussed:

(i') *Non-cognitivism*: No moral judgement just *is* a (true, or even false) statement of fact.

(ii') *Hume's gap*: No moral judgement can be deduced from a set of premisses made up exclusively of (true or false) statements of fact.

And earlier in that chapter I discussed:

(iii) *The naturalistic fallacy thesis*: No moral term (or property) can be *defined* (or analysed) exclusively in terms of naturalistic terms (or properties).

Now anyone who is a (i') non-cognitivist will (I think) have to hold (ii') as well. (This is a somewhat complex matter. See Snare 1977b.) Furthermore any (i') non-cognitivist will have to hold (iii) as well. So anyone who has a good argument for non-cognitivism will have good reasons for accepting the other two claims as well. But of course we have seen in chapter 5 that there is not all that much in the way of argument for non-cognitivism (perhaps the apparent poor running of the alternatives). But we might consider what *independent* reasons there might be for believing either (ii') or (iii), that is, apart from already believing (i').

HUME'S GAP: NO 'OUGHT' FROM 'IS'

Hume in his *Treatise* observed that writers on ethics typically make a certain unexplained transition. At first they are discussing what *is* the case in the world, but then suddenly they are discussing what *ought* to be the case. This transition, Hume said (perhaps with a little irony), needs to be explained. Now Hume was certainly right that there are a lot of bad, or at least suspicious, arguments from 'is' to 'ought' around. It is worth considering the mistakes they involve.

Let's consider one example. Some people seem to argue from 'Homosexuality is unnatural' to 'Homosexuality is wrong' or 'Homosexuality ought to be forbidden'. Now one of the problems with this particular argument is that 'unnatural' has a great many different meanings. The person employing this argument is seldom very clear what he means. Or else he jumps from sense to sense to reply to whatever is the most immediate objection. But, roughly, the proponent of this argument is in a kind of dilemma. In so far as 'natural' or 'unnatural' is given a more uncontroversially factual meaning (e.g. such as one the biological sciences might give it) it becomes less and less obvious that the 'ought' conclusion does follow. For example, if 'unnatural' means only 'statistically unusual, abnormal, or deviant', then hang-gliding and stamp-collecting will also turn out 'unnatural'. But who would then say they are immoral? Alternatively, the word 'unnatural' can be loaded with some moral or 'emotive' content. (The reason many would not call hang-gliding 'unnatural' is just that they are not *already* inclined to think it wrong.) In that case the inference from 'unnatural' to 'wrong' is perhaps valid (even if a little question-begging) but the premiss is no longer an uncontroversial case of an 'is' statement. It's more a case of deriving 'ought' from 'ought' (or 'ought not' from 'ought not').

Another thing that may happen is that an argument from 'is' to 'ought' may *look* valid, but only because certain further premisses, 'ought' premisses, have been assumed or suppressed. For example, the person who argues from 'x is in accordance with our human nature' to 'x is right for us' may be assuming as further premisses 'What is in accordance with one's nature leads to more happiness and less sorrow' and 'We *ought* to do what leads to happiness and avoids sorrow'. Here again, one of the premisses is an 'ought' premiss (and thus not an *uncontroversial* case of an 'is' premiss).

Now everyone agrees there are many bad, or shifty, inferences from 'is' to 'ought'. However, (ii'), Hume's gap thesis, claims rather more. It claims to know in advance of the examination of any particular alleged inference from 'is' to 'ought' (i.e. from any set of cognitive statements to a moral judgement) that it *must* fail, that it will not be valid! This amazingly self-assured thesis certainly requires an argument. It is not some uncontroversial truism (as many seem to have thought) but a profoundly sweeping generalization. In the light of this is it surprising that no philosopher has ever given a *direct* argument for the gap thesis? (An indirect argument would argue, independently, for (i') non-cognitivism, and then argue that (ii') Hume's gap was a logical consequence.)

But if no one has attempted to prove that gap thesis, has it ever been disproved? Are there any counter-examples, i.e. clear cases of valid inference from uncontroversially cognitive premises to an uncontroversially value conclusion? Well, some philosophers claim there are specific counter-examples of valid inference from facts to values (see Searle 1964; Foot 1958; Black 1966). Their arguments for this remain controversial, however.

I shall say no more about the ensuing controversy except to note that *one* (but not the only!) way in which we might produce a counter-example to (ii') is by employing a naturalistic definition. For example, suppose Aquinas is right that 'good for a species S' just means 'being naturally sought after by species S'. Then we could produce the following as a counter-example:

(a) Living in society is something humans (by their nature) seek after.

Therefore

(b) Living in society is a good thing for humans.

This is a valid argument *on the assumption* that Aquinas' definition (or analysis) is an adequate representation of what is meant by calling a thing 'good'. So we would refute both (ii'), Hume's gap, and (iii), the naturalistic fallacy, in one blow if we had some adequate naturalistic definition.

THE NATURALISTIC FALLACY: THE OPEN QUESTION ARGUMENT REOPENED

Unlike (ii'), Hume's gap thesis, (iii), the naturalistic fallacy thesis has been argued for *directly*. We have Moore's open question argument against any proposed naturalistic definition of a value term. Moore used this argument to try to get a quite sweeping conclusion. It wasn't just that one or two defective naturalistic definitions fell prey to this argument; Moore thought that for any proposed naturalistic definition a corresponding open question could always be produced which would refute it. But there are a couple of reasons for supposing that Moore failed to show anything so sweeping.

1 Multiple meanings

As a preliminary, let us note that *non-moral* goodness is the most plausible candidate for a naturalistic definition. Most naturalistic definitions of 'good' become rather more plausible if one assumes the good at issue is *non-moral* goodness. Thus it is not surprising that a great many naturalistic definitions of 'good' employ some motivational or psychological element (e.g. 'pleasure', 'desire', 'naturally seeking', 'desire to desire'). That some such definition may work seems very plausible if we are defining *non-moral* goodness. Of course my good (i.e. my non-moral good) is not simply whatever I desire, for I may sometimes want things or have whims that are, as I myself admit, (non-morally) bad for me (e.g. cigarettes, too much cholesterol). But that may be because at some deeper, more integrated, level of consciousness I desire to avoid, say, cancer or a heart attack. So perhaps a very complex naturalistic definition could be given in terms of deeper desires, 'natural' desires, long-term, integrated, 'on balance' desires, and/or perhaps in terms of what I *would* desire if I had a more vivid appreciation of consequences, or had more willpower, or could calculate probabilities better. For *non-moral* goodness, that seems quite plausible.

But even if there is such a successful definition of non-moral good, the corresponding Moorean question ('But are things with *that* rather complex motivational property good?') might nevertheless give the *appearance* of being 'open' and sensible, but only because we tend to switch tacitly to a different sense of 'good', i.e. *moral* goodness. (We are naturally given to a little generosity in our attempts to understand the questions of others and thus tend to construe their words in the ways which will make the most sense.) However, the question asked strictly in terms of *non-moral* goodness may *not* make sense. It may be a closed question – a question so conceptually odd we actually tend to suppose some other question is really the one being asked. Even Moore's paradigm of an open question ('It's pleasant but is it good?') might *seem* sensible, but only because we are implicitly assuming that the 'good' means '*morally* good'. The person who thinks that some, or all, pleasures are immoral, whether he is right or wrong, is at least *not* conceptually confused. That question is a real one. But it is not quite so obvious that it makes sense to ask whether something pleasant is *non-morally* good. Of course a given pleasure may not on balance be to one's (non-moral) good (if, to take only one case, it has a great many painful consequences). But the very fact that it has to be outweighed by these other considerations suggests that pleasantness in itself counts toward a thing's (non-moral) goodness. Would we really make much sense of a person who asked of something pleasant, not 'Is it good on balance?', but 'Is it good *at all*?' (where he meant '*non-morally* good')? Certainly it is not obvious that such a question is open. Those who think otherwise are perhaps either confusing this question with the quite different one posed in terms of *moral* goodness, or else are blind adherents of the Moorean dogma that any form of naturalism just *must* be fallacious.

In summary, we need to be very careful in employing the open question argument. A question can seem 'open', when it is not, just because we have unthinkingly switched to some other ordinary sense of one of the terms in the question – perhaps as a result of our natural charity in making sense out of what we hear uttered. I have also suggested that some fairly complex naturalistic definition of 'non-moral good', involving motivational or psychological elements, just might be a goer.

2 Analysis and the 'is' of composition

There is an even more fundamental reason for being suspicious about Moore's use of the open question argument. In the first few chapters I characterized meta-ethics as looking for answers to certain 'What is . . .?' questions (rather like the sort Socrates asked): 'What *is* goodness?', 'What *is* rightness?', 'What *is* it to think an act right?', 'What *is* it to make a moral judgement?'. I noted that 'is' in such questions was *not* the 'is' of *predication*. We are not asking (as ethical theory might) 'What various things *are* good (i.e. have the property of goodness)?', but rather 'What *is* the property of goodness?' This 'is' is the 'is' of *identity*.

However, there are still several different kinds of *identity* claims which can be made. U.T. Place (1956; see Smart 1959 and Churchland 1984: ch. 2, sec. 3), in connection with philosophy of mind rather than meta-ethics, distinguishes these two kinds of 'is' of identity: (a) the 'is' of definition, (b) the 'is' of composition. In the case of (a), the 'is' of definition, an identity claim is made on the basis of a definition of the terms involved (or on the basis of a conceptual analysis of the notions involved). For example, the property of being a vixen *is* the property of being a female fox. We would expect the knowledge of this identity to be delivered a priori.

On the other hand, we also make identity claims such as the following:

(i) The morning star *is* the evening star.
(ii) Clouds *are* masses of water droplets.
(iii) Lightning *is* electric discharges in the atmosphere.

These identity claims are not based purely on a priori conceptual investigations but have resulted from a posteriori scientific investigations and discoveries. Thus for two properties, P_1 and P_2, to be identical it is not necessary that 'P_1' and 'P_2' (the terms referring to these properties, respectively) be synonymous. 'Lightning' does not *mean* 'electrical discharges in the atmosphere'. Certainly the question 'That's lightning, but is there any electricity there?' is sensible and 'open'.

So I think it is possible for the naturalist to hold that when he says 'Goodness *is* N' he is not giving a definition or conceptual analysis of 'good'. He is not saying 'good' and 'N' are synonymous. Rather, he is identifying what property goodness is. He is telling us what it really is. For example, suppose there was good reason and evidence to believe Aquinas's account of the world and our place in it: he described the world as a hierarchy of things and living beings, striving by their various natures for a hierarchy of ends which are consistent and harmonious with each other. One could see the point, in such an event, of saying that good is to be identified with that which all things by nature aim at. Certainly it would be perverse to resist this identification simply on the grounds that 'good' does not *mean* 'being aimed at by all things'.

It has been fashionable in this century for meta-ethics to claim that 'What is . . .?' questions were purely matters of the definitional (i.e. analytical) 'is'. No doubt there are important and interesting linguistic or conceptual questions about the meaning of moral language and moral discourse. But the naturalist may not be making that sort of a priori 'is' claim, but a somewhat more a posteriori 'is' claim. If so, the naturalist's claim is not refuted by Moore's open question argument, for that at most shows that the identity is not a *definitional* one.

The consequences

1 Naturalism has been resurrected. It has not been refuted by Moore if we assume the naturalist intends his 'is' of identity to be compositional rather than definitional.

2 Non-cognitivism is not in quite so strong a position as it seemed before, given that one of the reasons for accepting non-cognitivism was the apparent failure of the main alternatives, including naturalism. But naturalism, it seems, might make a comeback.

3 On the other hand non-cognitivist theories such as emotivism may also be in a somewhat better position as regarding some of the objections made against them. When the emotivist says that making a moral judgement just is expressing attitudes and exhorting others to have them as well, he need not be making a definitional identity claim. Rather, he might be saying that, given what we know about human nature and the world, it turns out that that is what making a moral judgement really amounts to. This may even come as something of a surprise to those who use moral discourse and make moral judgements (as surprising as discovering that lightning really is electricity).

FURTHER READING

Basic reading on 'Hume's gap' includes Frankena (1930: 468–77) and the essays collected in Hudson (1970). Foot (1958) and Richards (1980: ch. 2) argue for the existence of the gap, while Searle (1964) and Black (1966) launch a limited counter-attack. Stove (1978) is useful for removing certain common misunderstandings, while Snare (1977a) is a useful reference.

The open question test is critically discussed in Brandt (1959: 155–66; 1979), and forcefully disputed in Churchland (1984), Smart (1959), and Place (1956). Hancock (1960) contends that the test is circular and only seems effective on the basis of dubious metaphysics, while Snare (1975c) defends a novel reading of Moore's question as a linguistic, not metaphysical, test.

7

Relativism in general

Chapters 8–11 will examine the various things that might be meant by saying that morality is in some way relative or else subjective. However, in those chapters the assumption will be that those who say that morality is relative are making a discriminating claim. A *discriminating* relativist about morality thinks that morality is relative in a sense that contrasts interestingly with other areas of belief (e.g. core science) which are not relative. But another kind of relativist thinks morality is relative for the much more basic reason that he thinks *everything* is relative. Thus some people are drawn to the view that morality is relative simply because they are indiscriminate relativists. An *indiscriminate* relativist thinks that all truth (or all reality) is relative, the relativity of morals being only a particular instance of what goes on globally.

These two kinds of ways of thinking morality relative are importantly different in their force and consequences. While indiscriminate relativism is a much more radical position than discriminating relativism, it is also one which reduces much of the sting in the claim that morality is relative. For if *everything* is relative, there is no longer any reason to suppose some great metaphysical gap between morality and, say, science. Morality can't be too badly off if it is no worse than contemporary chemistry or biology in that regard. For this reason discussion of the relativism with more bite, discriminating relativism, will concern us in the later chapters. The present chapter is concerned solely with relativism of the indiscriminate, or global, sort. This does take us into issues and arguments that belong more to metaphysics and epistemology than to moral philosophy in particular. But this cannot be avoided. For one thing, some people really do think morality is relative just because everything is relative. Or at least the arguments they give for thinking morality relative, if they work at all, could just as well be used to show anything else relative. For another thing, we will not really be able in the later chapters to understand what discriminating relativism holds until we understand the indiscriminate relativism which it rejects and the special difficulties encountered by the latter but not the former.

PROTAGORAS' THEORY OF TRUTH

The place to begin in the discussion of global (i.e. indiscriminate) relativism is with the difficulties raised by Socrates in Plato's dialogue *Theaetetus*. While this dialogue is really about knowledge, in the course of the discussion Socrates finds it necessary to examine the position of the sophist Protagoras, who held that 'Man is the measure'. Protagoras seems to have held that truth is relative, that whatever seems or appears so to someone *is* so (for that person). This seems to have been a version of global relativism. It is not the only version. Indeed there are many contemporary versions put forward by philosophers with much more sophistication. But it is always worth asking whether some appropriately modified form of Socrates' objection doesn't work in these other cases as well. Socrates' argument against Protagoras is one of those classic arguments (like the *Euthyphro* argument and Butler's argument) of which no student in philosophy should be ignorant. In each case the argument is not the last word on the subject (there are perhaps replies), but it cannot simply be ignored. Initially, at least, it shifts the burden of argument onto its opponents.

Protagoras does not appear in the dialogue, for good historical and dramatic reasons – at the time the dialogue is set he had been dead many years. Instead, his views are taken up by Theaetetus, a young mathematician, and Theodorus, an old mathematician. And when these flag, Socrates himself temporarily takes the side of Protagoras, if only so that the most charitable interpretation can be what is then subjected to criticism. Protagoras' famous catch-phrase for his doctrine was: Man is the measure of all things; man (i.e. humans or humankind – for the Greek word is unambiguously generic) is the measure of the existence of things that are, and of the nonexistence of things that are not. Protagoras put forward his doctrine in a book called *Truth*. Since that book has been lost, we more or less have to rely on Plato's report of it in the present dialogue. It appears from Plato's dialogue (*Theaet.*

152a) that Protagoras explained his view thus: Things *are* (to you) such as they appear (to you).

Here is an example that applies his view. Suppose one person is cold while a second has a fever. Also, a wind is blowing. Protagoras' view is not simply that the wind *feels* warm to one person and cold to the other (hardly a controversial view), but that it *is* these two ways. Or, more precisely, it *is warm* (to the cold person) while it *is cold* (to the fevered person). This particular example probably gives Protagoras' view more initial plausibility than it deserves. 'Warm' and 'cold' are rather special predicates. Philosophers typically class the properties these terms refer to among the 'secondary qualities'. (Another such property is colour.) An object has a given secondary quality in virtue of its power to produce, standardly, some appropriate experience in us (e.g. feeling warm, feeling cold). While controversial even here, Protagoras' story is more seemingly plausible in the very special case of secondary qualities.

However, Protagoras' claim is very much more controversial than the above, specially tailored, example suggests. Protagoras' view extends quite generally and is not at all restricted to the secondary qualities. Roughly, his view is that for any person A and any proposition p, if A believes that p, then p *is true* (for A). The proposition p might be about anything whatsoever and is not restricted to propositions attributing secondary qualities. More precisely, we might break his view down into the following components:

(1) 'True-for' relativity: (a) There is no such thing as a proposition's being *true* (full stop) any more than there is such a thing as a proposition's being *false* (full stop). (b) Instead, there is only a proposition's being *true-for-A*, *false-for-B*, *true-for-C*, etc.
(2) The criterion of 'true-for': The sole thing that can make a proposition p *true-for-A* is that A believe that p.

While this formulation is somewhat more elaborate than anything we find in the dialogue, it does have the advantage of setting forth precisely how Protagoras shares some claims with the philosophical relativists of today, and in what important ways he differs. Claim (1) above is what Protagoras would seem to share with all, or at least most, contemporary relativists. They are all in some way critical of what they consider to be our naïve ordinary notion of truth. However, unlike Protagoras, it is no longer fashionable (perhaps Socrates is responsible for this) to make truth relative to individual persons. The more recent forms of relativism have much larger canvases. According to them truth is relative, not to mere individuals, but to rather more social and historical entities, such as 'conceptual frameworks', 'language games', 'forms of life', 'scientific paradigms', or 'scientific revolutions'. Particularly to the short-sighted, a truth that is relative to one of these grander socio-historical entities might not seem all that different from an old-fashioned (full stop) sort of truth. That's a definite advantage for the contemporary versions, for they can claim to be in certain respects much less radical, and much closer to ordinary views about truth, than is Protagoras' view.

Claim (2) above is more peculiarly Protagorean. It makes truth relative to humans (or more precisely to believers). Claim (1) as it stands is an incomplete theory of the relativity of truth. It gives us no clue as to what sorts of things truth is relative to. It needs to be supplemented with some criterion of (relative) truth. That is precisely what Protagoras gives us in (2). That claim should not be misunderstood. It is not some linguistic proposal to use a new jargon phrase where we have a perfectly good ordinary term already. In particular, it is not the boring proposal that '*true-for*' be a jargon term for 'is believed by'. Rather, Protagoras is putting forth a theory of truth, relative truth to be sure, and presenting *belief* as the sole mark of such relative truth. In the following discussion I will speak of Protagoras' view in this short-hand fashion:

Protagoras' doctrine: Whatever a person believes is *true-for-that-person*.

However, in putting it this way claims (1) and (2) must still be supposed as a background. Belief is not just one, but the sole, mark of *truth-for*-hood – as per (2). And further, as per (1), there is only *truth-for*-hood. There is never truth (full stop).

FOUR PRELIMINARY OBJECTIONS

Before giving his main argument Socrates presents four preliminary objections. These do not refute Protagorean relativism, for replies can be given in each case. But the very process of defending Protagoras against the objection at the same time reveals how much more radical his view has to be than it might at first have appeared. These objections refine rather than refute.

1 The objection from dreams, madness, deceptions of the senses (157d–158e)

This is a kind of naïve, common-sense objection. What about dreams? What about madness? What about deceptions of the senses? Don't we ordinarily say that in such instances a person has beliefs (e.g. what he dreams, hallucinates), but that these beliefs are false? Such beliefs are just not true, not even for the person who has them.

We don't know how Protagoras would have replied to this objection. But at 158b Socrates suggests a reply on Protagoras' behalf. He argues that we have no way of determining whether we are dreaming or awake (and presumably no way of knowing when we are mad, or, when deceived by the senses, that we are being deceived). Interestingly enough, exactly the same difficulty is used by Descartes in the *First Meditation*. Descartes claims that we have no 'certain marks' to distinguish dreaming and waking. Some philosophers have questioned this claim, but let us suppose it is true. How can this claim be used to defend Protagoras against the present common-sense objection? Perhaps Protagoras is being made to argue thus:

(1) There is no certain way to *distinguish* dreaming from waking.

Therefore

(2) There *is* no distinction between dreaming and waking. (Everything is as it appears.)

However, it is important to see that this is just an invalid argument. That we are unable to distinguish one thing from another may only indicate a human defect. There may still be a distinction there even if we poor beings cannot distinguish it. Of course *one* possible explanation of our inability to distinguish is that there is no distinction to start with. But that is not the only possible explanation. Thus the premiss does not *prove* the conclusion. Even if no one can be sure whether he at present belongs to the class of dreamers or to the class of those awake, it would still count sufficiently against Protagoras' view that there are these two classes, that there are (or could be) some dreamers, i.e. people with false (full stop) beliefs. Whether we poor humans can determine with certainty who exactly these people are is just a separate matter.

But if the above is a bad reply on Protagoras' behalf, that is not to say there are no good replies. A defender of Protagoras might point out that the argument from dreams, madmen, etc. *begs the question* against Protagoras. A 'dreamer', under the ordinary, common-sense conception, is someone whose perceptions are *false* (full stop). A 'madman' is a person who typically has many *false* (full stop) beliefs. Again, to be 'deceived' by the senses is to perceive things *falsely*. To use any of these notions is already to presuppose the common-sense, non-relativist notion of truth. Hence Protagoras' response *should* be just to reject all these common-sense notions and to replace them with relativized notions of 'dreamer', 'awake', 'mad', 'sane', etc. On this view, no one is just mad (full stop). Instead, we must say, for instance, that A is mad-for-B but is sane-for-C and, quite likely, sane-for-A. Again, no one is just dreaming (full stop). Instead, A is dreaming-for-B but awake-for-A. And so on.

This reply not only saves Protagoras, it seems to me what his view in consistency demands. At this point it might seem as though this first objection has accomplished nothing against Protagoras. But that is not quite so. It has revealed something. One cannot just unravel the common-sense notion of truth (full stop) and leave it at that. A great many other common-sense concepts which presuppose that notion unravel at the same time. Indeed, very little of the fabric of common sense will be left. Only rarely does the relativist have the luxury of just taking common-sense notions for granted. More usually, he must replace them with suitably relativized notions. And we may well wonder whether what he undertakes to weave will hold together.

2 Man or pig objection (161c–d)

Socrates asks why Protagoras says that *humankind* is the measure. Why not pig the measure? Or baboon the measure? Or tadpole the measure? Isn't this just human chauvinism? Isn't it quite arbitrary, indeed anthropocentric, to pick out human beliefs as the measure if, as seems plausible, animals have beliefs too? Socrates is right here. Protagoras can give no reason why human beliefs should be singled out in this way. However, Socrates' success here is not all that important if Protagoras can plausibly adjust his position so as to avoid the present criticism. Unfortunately, the historical Protagoras formulated his position with the famous slogan that man is the measure. But Protagoras could just as well have said that all believers are measures. If other animals have beliefs, then what they believe will be true-for-them. Actually, we initially formulated Protagoras' criterion of true-for, not in terms of human beliefs, but in terms of beliefs generally. This was anticipating the present adjustment.

3 The wisdom of the gods objection (162c–e)

If Protagoras' theory applies generally to all believers then it applies to the gods. And the ordinary Greek, at least, would have no trouble admitting that the gods exist. But then Socrates raises this objection. On Protagoras' theory the gods have no more claim to wisdom than we do. They are no wiser than us. If it seems to us that p while it seems to the gods that not-p, then p is true-for-us while not-p is true-for-the-gods. There is no question of the gods getting it right (full stop!) more often then we do. At 162c Socrates gives Protagoras a reply to this objection. Protagoras is made to say that the question of the existence of the gods is something 'I banish from writing and speech'. Apparently he refused to discuss the issue. On the face of it that just seems like an unphilosophical evasion rather than an adequate response to the present objection. Perhaps Protagoras' secret view was that the gods do not exist. But then there is a problem for Protagoras. Given that Protagoras does not believe in the gods, then, on the relativist view, they do not exist *for Protagoras*. But if anyone else believes in the gods, then, on the relativist view, the gods do exist *for those who so believe*.

I think consistency demands a different sort of reply from Protagoras. I would have expected Protagoras at this point to reject any absolute (non-relativized) notions of 'gods' or 'wisdom'. While the Greeks may not have thought their gods all-knowing, they did commonly believe that the gods know a bit more than we do of the truth (full stop). And for that matter the ordinary notion of wisdom involves knowing something of what is true (full stop). What Protagoras should say is that his theory rejects these common-sense, non-relativized notions of 'gods' or 'wisdom' or 'know', just as it must reject the non-relativized notions of 'dreamer' or 'madness'. One is a god, or wise, or a knower for those who believe one is, but not for those who believe otherwise. One is never just a god, or wise, or a knower (full stop). As we saw before, one cannot relativize the notion of truth without also relativizing a great many other notions which are entangled with that concept.

4 The wisdom of Protagoras (161c–162a)

This fourth objection is no more philosophically penetrating than the first three. But it's one that must hit Protagoras where it hurts a sophist most – in the wallet. It's a beautiful *ad hominem*. If what appears to a person is true (for that person), then what becomes of Protagoras' alleged wisdom? And if Protagoras is no wiser (full stop) than anyone else, why should his students pay him? As Socrates puts it, if each person is the sole judge and whatever one judges is true-for-oneself, then why should Protagoras be thought particularly wise and deserve to be well paid? Is not the 'ignoramus' as much a measure of his own truth as Protagoras?

It's worth reflecting at this point that these four arguments are really only different ways of making the same general point. We ordinarily distinguish those awake from those dreaming, those sane from those mad, those perceiving veridically from those deceived by their senses. Again, we think humans are, on the whole, a level above pigs or baboons. Similarly, the gods are a level above humans. Finally, we suppose that reputable teachers are, on the whole, a level above their students in regard to the subject matter of instruction. That is, in each case we think the former class is, on the whole, wiser in some respect or respects than the latter class. To put it in the language of chapter 2 above, we might say that the ordinary view is that the former has some 'authority' in the epistemic sense. That is, the former is better placed, epistemically, to know the truth (full stop). Now, I have suggested that the consistent relativist reply to this general sort of objection must be to reject these ordinary distinctions and their implicit commitment to a non-relativized notion of truth. In effect, the relativist must reject that there ever are 'authorities' in the epistemic sense. No one is better placed than another to know the truth. Each person is the sole measure of what is true for that person. Indeed the relativist view seems to be that *everyone* is an authority, not in the epistemic sense, but in the empowerment sense. It's not that I discover what is already true, but that I actually make it true (for me at least), just by believing it.

And this suggests that there might be some kind of Euthyphro-type difficulty for Protagoras' view. That is not to say that Socrates actually raises any such difficulty in the *Theaetetus*. But it's an instructive exercise to consider whether there might not be some such difficulty. The problem must go something like this. If Protagoras' view is correct, can it ever be possible for us to form beliefs on rational grounds? There is, of course, no special problem where one has prior irrational (or even non-rational) beliefs. The belief, however irrationally founded, makes it so (for oneself, at least). One can always be sure of an amnesty, after the fact. But what about the case where one has no prior belief, where indeed one is trying to form one's belief on rational grounds? Here one is in effect asking what is the truth (or, at least, the truth-for-me). But Protagoras' criterion of truth stipulates that the only ground for my truth is my prior believing it to be true. But there is no prior belief in the case where I am specifically trying to form my beliefs on rational grounds. Protagoras' theory is one which, if believed, must paralyse rational belief formation. A god dedicated to commanding action only on the basis of his prior rational belief that the act is moral will be paralysed once he sees that it is only his commanding that makes any act right. Likewise a person dedicated to forming a belief only on rational grounds will be paralysed once that person sees that those grounds can only be one's already having the belief in question. Of course, if one can somehow irrationally induce the belief, then what is believed will become true-for-one. Automatic amnesties, afterwards. But this requires, temporarily at least, something other than rational belief formation. If Protagoras' theory is correct, it will be a mistake to think too much about one's beliefs. Reflective belief formation will always consist in plotting against oneself. Of course a relativist might reply on behalf of Protagoras that that is just the way things are. Fully rational and reflective belief formation is not possible. And is this surprising? Just as there can, on this view, be no epistemic authorities or experts or wisdom, so there can be no such thing as rationality in belief formation. One's beliefs are never to be measured against some prior standard of rationality; one's beliefs are themselves the sole measure of what *is* (for oneself).

THE PRAGMATIC DEFENCE OF RELATIVISM
(166d–168c)

The defence of Protagoras' view suggested above makes it a consistent but rather bleak view. It is clearly something very far from common sense. Socrates suggests a quite different defence of Protagoras against the four objections. It is interesting because it brings Protagoras' view much closer in line with common sense. It also suggests, unlike the above, that we might not after all be fools to pay Protagoras for his instruction. Finally, it is of interest because it is very usual for relativists not to grasp the nettle of strict consistency in the manner I have suggested but instead to rest their relativism on a more fundamental *pragmatism*. And in many ways this really makes relativism a more plausible thesis. Hence Socrates' account of Protagoras' defence is in some ways more sympathetic than the one I have suggested above.

Protagoras' reply to the why-is-Protagoras-so-wise objection (as presented by Socrates) is this. There is a distinction between those who are wise and those who are not. But the distinction is not a matter of the former knowing truths (full stop) which the latter miss. The sophist's wisdom consists, not in substituting true beliefs for false beliefs, but in substituting *better* beliefs for *worse*. Here we are not told exactly what 'betterness' consists in. There could be a great many different versions: what makes one feel better, what is in one's interest, what allows one to get on socially, what is socially functional, what has good social consequences, etc.

Notice that the move here is not, as before, just to abandon ordinary distinctions and conceptions, but rather to try to reconstruct and account for them. Protagoras is here trying to account for our normal distinction between wise and ignorant (and perhaps even our ordinary distinction between true and false) by saying that, while there is no real distinction between true and false, there is a real distinction between better and worse beliefs. There is after all a distinction, even if it is a pragmatic rather than a metaphysical one. No one's beliefs are any truer than anyone else's. But some might be more useful or valuable to have (indeed worth paying for). Standing back a bit, we can appreciate a certain irony in this present 'pragmatic turn'. We began the chapter considering that one way to defend the view that morality and values are relative is to derive value relativism from relativism in general.

But, when pushed, the present version of general relativism rests in turn on prior claims about values, about what it is better for one to believe. We seem to have come in some sort of circle.

In a later section we shall see that Socrates has an objection that is particularly devastating for most attempts to base relativism on pragmatism. But for the present we might consider a certain dilemma. The following is the sort of thing the pragmatic relativist wants to assert:

q: Believing p is *better* for one than believing not-p.

Now the thing to ask about the above proposition q is whether it is itself true (full stop) or whether, like all else, it is merely true for those who believe it. There are problems either way. If q, unlike all else, just is true (full stop), then it turns out that even Protagoras' theory of truth has some absolute truths. And, rather implausibly, it is certain moral or value claims which turn out to be absolutely true. In this case the appeal to pragmatism must give up global relativism. On the other hand, suppose proposition q is only true for those who believe it, and false for those who disbelieve it. In that case (and somewhat more consistently) 'better' and 'useful' become just as relative as 'true'. One consequence of this will be that the claim that Protagoras is wise will only be true for those who believe that Protagoras' beliefs are better for one to believe. Protagoras will not be wise for those who think otherwise about the utility of his beliefs. In this case the appeal to pragmatism does not really take us closer to common sense. We might as well be back with one of the austere versions of relativism which makes no concessions to common sense.

THE PERITROPE (168d–171d)

Socrates' main criticism is, if it works, a particularly destructive sort of criticism. It is not a criticism of arguments for Protagoras' relativism. Indeed, unlike the case with most modern versions of relativism, we have no idea what arguments Protagoras had in favour of his view (unless, perhaps, it was some misleading observations about secondary qualities). But Socrates' criticism aims to be much more devastating. It aims to show that the relativist thesis turns on itself. The Greek term 'peritrope' can mean 'a turning back on one'. A suggestive image is that of a snake continuing to devour its own tail. Socrates thinks Protagoras' theory does not need outside criticism. It devours itself. And the argument he gives to show this has come to be called 'the peritrope'.

Actually, Socrates gives three versions of the peritrope. The basic idea is the same, but each version increases in generality and makes the point more powerfully. The first, and most modest, version goes like this. Notice that most ordinary people implicitly reject Protagoras' relativism. For example, most people think they are experts on certain subject matters but that others are experts on other things. Even Protagoras thinks that your ordinary ignoramus has beliefs of this form: B believes that A has a belief that is false (full stop). It is common to think that someone else has just got it wrong. And it needn't even be another person. B could be my present self and A could be my past self. It is not unusual to believe now that some of one's past beliefs were simply false. Indeed, if Protagoras did not think people commonly believed this sort of absolutist nonsense he could not think his own relativist theory was news to them. This fact about ordinary people serves as the first premiss in the *first version* of the peritrope:

(1) B believes that A has a belief that is false (full stop) [fact about people].
(2) Whatever a person believes is true-for-that-person [Protagoras' doctrine].

Therefore

(3) It is true-for-B that A has a false (full stop) belief.

Hence Protagoras must accept the conclusion. What the argument shows is that even from the standpoint of Protagoras' theory there is, in a way, such a thing as a false (full stop) belief. That is, there is such a thing as long as it gets relativized to someone else's beliefs about them. Protagoras must say that there are false (full stop) beliefs for those ordinary people who believe there are such false beliefs. The conclusion does not refute Protagoras, of course. But it shows that Protagoras' theory must make a certain concession to (full stop) true and false beliefs. It also sets the stage for the second version of the argument.

We may be more specific. Not only do ordinary people think a lot of the beliefs of others are simply false, more particularly they think this of Protagoras' theory. Most people do not accept Protagoras' doctrine. And Protagoras must concede this too, for his teaching is intended to overthrow just this ordinary prejudice.

And this provides us with the first premiss of the *second version* of the peritrope:

(1) Most people believe that Protagoras' theory is false [fact about people].
(2) What a person believes to be false is false-for-that-person [Protagoras' theory].

Therefore

(3) Protagoras' theory is false-for-most-people.

Thus, on his own theory of truth, and given that most do not already accept it, it follows that the theory itself is false for those many who do not accept it.

The second version of the peritrope shows that Protagoras' theory is false from the point of view of most. The *third version* twists the blade one more turn. It shows that even from Protagoras' point of view his theory is false for most people. We may conveniently divide this version into two parts:

(1) Protagoras *believes* that most people *believe* Protagoras' theory of truth is false [fact explaining why Protagoras teaches].
(2) What a person believes to be false is false-for-that-person [Protagoras' theory].

Therefore

(3) Protagoras *believes* that his own theory of truth is false-for-most-people.

We may then use this conclusion, (3), as our first premiss, along with premiss (2) again, to get:

(3) Protagoras *believes* that his own theory of truth is false-for-most-people.
(2) What a person believes to be false is false-for-that-person [Protagoras' theory].

Therefore

(4) It is true-for-Protagoras that his theory of truth is false-for-most.

One now wonders why Protagoras is so concerned to proselytize his theory. Even on his own grounds, his theory is false for all those others who don't believe it. A thoroughgoing relativist theory relativizes even itself. It gives no special advantage to itself over absolutist theories of truth. Certainly it cannot say the relativist theory is *true* while the absolutist theory is *false*. Or at any rate, a relativist who says something like that has altered his relativism in a quite radical way. What such a relativist now says is that while *most* truth is relative there are nevertheless a few absolute truths, e.g. that most truth is relative. However, once it is conceded that the notion of 'true' (full stop) has even this one proper employment, the difference between the relativist and the rest of us is not quite so radical. Furthermore, this modified sort of relativism has double the task of any ordinary theory of truth, for it must explain *two* notions of truth ('true' and 'true-for-one'), what their relationships might be, and just why the line gets drawn where it does between those things which are true in the relativistic way and those which are true (full stop).

Finally, we might tie this discussion of the relativity of truth to questions about the relativity of morality. Notice that just as relativism about truth tends to dissolve itself (as the versions of the peritrope show), so also relativism about truth tends to dissolve the force of any claim that morality is relative. Suppose someone is a relativist about morality. We take such a person to be asserting things like 'Act A is right relative to moral code x but is wrong relative to moral code y'. Now doesn't the interesting force of this claim come from our assumption that this moral relativist means to say that it is *true* (full stop) that the act is right relative to one code but wrong relative to another? We take the claim to be that it is *true* (full stop) that morality is relative. But let us now suppose the moral relativist is also a relativist about truth. This has the effect of very much diluting the force of the moral relativism. Like Protagoras, all that can be said is that 'Morality is relative' is true-for-those who believe it is while at the same time 'Morality is absolute' is true-for-those (rather more) who believe it is not relative. It would appear that relativism about truth is much too even-handed between moral relativism and moral absolutism. The more robust forms of moral relativism will reject relativism about truth.

PREDICTIONS ABOUT OUR OWN FUTURES

In the face of the difficulties raised by Socrates' peritrope argument, it may seem even more attractive to rest relativism about truth on pragmatism. Propositions (such as 'Morality is relative', 'Truth is relative') are not *true* (full stop), but it may be that believing them is more useful, more in one's interest, better for one. Some beliefs just 'work better'. By contrast, the consistent relativism of Protagoras can, as Socrates' argument shows, only seem barren and self-defeating. But a pragmatic relativism seems capable of giving guidance, even if that guidance is based on utility rather than truth.

The problem for pragmatic relativism is a somewhat different one. Judgements about what will be useful, what will work, what will be better, involve predictions. Perhaps one of Socrates' most powerful arguments brings out the problem relativism has with predictions (178b–c). Socrates considers this case: Suppose someone makes a judgement about what *will* seem hot to him in the future. In a common-sense sort of way Socrates asks whether the person is the sole measure of this. Wouldn't we normally think there is such a thing as being mistaken in this prediction? For example, when an ordinary person thinks he is going to have a fever but a trained physician thinks the contrary, who is likely to be right? I suppose Protagoras will say that it is just relative. It is true-for-the-person that he will have a fever but false-for-the-physician that the patient will have a fever. So far this argument is just the usual stand off between common sense (which accepts the notion of expertise) and Protagoras' consistent relativism.

But we may give the argument a further twist. Even in my own case, and without bringing in the physician, don't I think there is such a thing as making a mistaken prediction about my own future? Perhaps in the future I won't believe what I believe now, or I won't feel the fever which I think I'll feel, or it won't at the time taste as I now think it will taste. Now what Protagoras cannot say here is that my present belief turns out to be *false*. Instead, consistency demands that the conflict between the belief of my present self and the belief of my future self be handled in exactly the same way as the conflict in beliefs between the patient and his physician. No one is the expert. No one is mistaken. But what we see more clearly now is that, because beliefs are held at particular times and can change over time, the true measure of truth is not the individual person but rather the person at a given time. The real measures of truth (the holders of beliefs) are what we might call 'person–time-slices'. Hence the consistent relativist view about the fever case will be (where P is the person, t_1 is now and t_2 is a later time):

(i) Because P-at-t_1 believes that P will be hot at t_2, then 'P is hot at t_2' is true-for-P-at-t_1.

But

(ii) Because P-at-t_2 doesn't feel hot, then 'P is hot at t_2' is false-for-P-at-t_2.

In the context of Protagorean relativism there can be no non-arbitrary reason for treating the beliefs of our future selves any differently from the beliefs of others.

This further relativization (to person–time-slices) has two important implications. First, we now see that relativism dissociates us from our own futures. Relativized truth is not just a matter of true-for-me (as opposed to false-for-you). It is more precisely a matter of true-for-me-*now* (as opposed to false-for-me-*later*). But second, this further relativization undermines the turn to pragmatism which does much to make relativism seem less implausible. Relativism about truth can be made to seem less removed from ordinary practical views by enlisting notions like 'useful belief', 'better belief', 'works', etc. But the problem is that, in so far as one's judgements about what 'works', or what will be better, involve predictions about how one will feel or believe or be in the future, those predictions can only be true or false relative to one's present self. What is true or false for some future self cannot bear on what is true for me now. The future person is just another person. What is true-for-me-now is that my having a certain belief will be useful for me because that is what I *now* believe. But there is no independent test of the truth of this prediction about my future states. All my predictions are true-for-*me-now*, just because I now believe them. Relativism dissolves the pragmatic test just as it dissolves its own force.

RECENT EXAMPLES OF RELATIVISM

Protagoras' theory of relative truth is forthright, but perhaps not as sophisticated as contemporary versions of relativism. Today relativists are less inclined to make truth relative to individuals (much less person–time-slices), but instead tend to speak of conceptual frameworks, forms of life, languages, scientific paradigms, and so on. Their relativism tends to be more historical and sociological than individualistic. Consider this quotation from a recent, quite engaging, book: 'In mediaeval Europe, witches really inhabited the common-sense world while in modern times they do not, although a number of types of psychiatrically sick people do' (Chalmers 1976: 131). Chalmers does not now hold any form of a relative theory of truth. Perhaps he never did. But it is a useful exercise to consider what the above sentence might mean. A natural way of interpreting this passage is that there exist certain *belief frameworks*. One such framework is the common-sense world of medieval Europe. Another is the contemporary scientific world view. Now, there are a couple of ways of taking this sentence which in no way implies relativism about truth. First, it might be no more than historical explanation. One culture believes in witches where the other sees only psychiatrically sick persons. This difference in belief might in the end have to be explained by deep differences in the conceptual frameworks of the two cultures. But notice that such an *explanation* of belief differences is compatible with there being some (full stop) truth on the matter. Perhaps some belief frameworks (e.g. the contemporary scientific world view) really are more adequate to the truth than others. That we can explain belief differences does not make truth relative. Second, there might be a hint of epistemological scepticism in the above passage. Perhaps we poor humans can never *know* or have any good reason to think one framework is better than another. But even this kind of scepticism does not imply relativism. There still could be (full stop) truth. One belief framework might in fact be more adequate than another. Our inability to discern such things would be merely a failing in us.

Rather, a theory of truth relative to belief frameworks would look something like this. First, there are certain belief frameworks, certain general outlooks upon the world, certain general ways of viewing the world. One example is the common-sense world of medieval Europe. Another is the contemporary scientific world view. Second, the truth of everyday, ground-level propositions is relative to these frameworks. For example, it is true relative to the common-sense world of medieval Europe that certain persons are witches. But this is false relative to the contemporary scientific world view. What is true relative to that view is that persons like that are psychiatrically sick. Notice that this kind of relativism is not nearly as extreme as Protagoras', precisely because the relativity is not to the individual's beliefs but to current socially held belief frameworks. Thus mere individuals such as you or I can have beliefs that are mistaken, if they are not warranted by the current belief framework of our society. The framework is the measure.

However, there are several claims involved in framework relativism whose status is far from clear. Here are three. First, there is the claim that certain *particular* frameworks exist and have existed. Shall we say, for example, that the claim that the medieval world view existed is true (full stop)? If so, it would seem that second-order claims about what belief frameworks have existed in the past are simply *true* (even if ground-level claims about witches, etc. are only true relative to frameworks). This seems to assume that the belief framework of twentieth-century historical research (which talks about the 'medieval world view') has got it right while other cultures rather more deficient in historical understanding have less adequate views. Or shall we say that the claim 'The medieval world view existed' is only true relative to our contemporary scientific framework? Second, there is the *general* claim that belief frameworks exist and have existed. But notice that the very notion of a belief framework is not to be found in most cultures and is a very peculiar feature of our culture. Is this claim that belief frameworks exist true (full stop)? If so, belief frameworks (like Chalmers') which include the notion of 'belief framework' are superior to those which have no place for the notion. Or is the claim only that belief frameworks exist relative to *our* belief framework, while 'belief frameworks' do not exist relative to others? And finally, we may ask Socrates' question again. Is the whole theory that truth is relative to frameworks itself true? Or, as in the peritrope, is it only true relative to our contemporary framework? Indeed, is it even true relative to that? The notion of (full stop) truth seems so embedded in our current scientific outlook that someone who speaks of truth relative to frameworks must seem like a revolutionary attempting to change our contemporary framework, rather than one who appeals to what we already have.

This chapter has been concerned to show that the place to begin in any investigation of relativism is with Socrates' arguments in the *Theaetetus*. But it is only the beginning. Socrates began a dialogue which continues unabated today. Indeed, in recent philosophy we find something of a resurgence of various subtle forms of relativism (or what seem to be relativism), along with, of course, vigorous counter-arguments by philosophical critics. But Socrates' argument at least shifts the burden of proof. Any credible form of relativism must be able to show that it overcomes the difficulties Socrates raised.

FURTHER READING

Of course the place to begin is with the primary source, Plato's *Theaetetus*. A useful article on Socrates' argument is Burnyeat (1976). For those interested in a closer study there is the recent commentary on the *Theaetetus* by McDowell (1973). For an argument that relativism is not self-refuting see Hesse (1980: ch. 2).

In contemporary philosophy relativism about truth is typically associated with other forms of relativism: about reason and rationality, about knowledge, about concepts, and even about perception. A useful recent anthology containing articles on all sides is Hollis and Lukes (1982). Influential recent works with a strong relativistic bent are Kuhn (1970) and Feyerabend (1975). The idea of a conceptual scheme is criticized in Davidson (1973–4), while what truth there may be in relativism is taken up by Williams (1974–5). Ontological relativity is discussed in Quine (1969).

A closely related topic is how, or indeed *whether*, it is possible to understand another culture and translate their language. A classic discussion is Whorf (1956). See also Winch (1958; 1964). Some influential philosophical theses bearing on this issue are Quine's 'indeterminacy of translation' thesis (1960), the Kuhn–Feyerabend 'incommensurability' thesis, and Davidson's 'principle of charity' (1973–4).

8

Descriptive relativism and
meta-ethical subjectivism

In chapters 5 and 6 I discussed the three main kinds of meta-ethical theories (naturalism, non-naturalism, non-cognitivism) as well as some of the arguments for and against each kind. I shall not consider what further arguments have been given for any of the further instances of such theories which have been proposed. Such is the subject matter of more advanced studies. Instead, chapters 8 through 11 will be concerned to clear up certain common misunderstandings people have about the leading meta-ethical theories (especially non-cognitivism). Meta-ethical theories are often thought to have consequences (sometimes practical consequences) which they do not.

MORALIZING AGAINST MORALIZING

Non-cognitivist theories (but also *certain* naturalist ones) can *seem* very radical and upsetting. They can make it look as if morality is 'only subjective' or 'all relative'. I somewhat dislike using words like 'subjective' or 'relative' because they are often used with no clear meaning. (Nor are their opposites much more helpful. 'Objective'? 'Absolute'? Such terms do not seem to gain their popular meanings from their role in any everyday practical activity or judgement. They are more likely to pop up in pubs or at parties where garrulous people are waxing 'philosophical'.)

While those who throw around pseudo-jargon terms like 'subjective' or 'relative' usually can't explain what they mean, the same people tend to say other things as well which do seem to play a certain practical role (more than just trying to impress others with jargon). Here are some examples of things said:

   (i) 'Nothing is just right or wrong, full stop. What is wrong-for-you might be right-for-me, or vice versa.'
  (ii) 'One is never really in a position to protest against someone with a different moral view.'
 (iii) 'We all have to make our own choices. No one can tell anyone else what is right or wrong.'

Such sentences, as we shall see, have a great many different meanings. But whatever they might mean, I *suspect* that such sentences are frequently used with the intention of getting certain practical results. However, the practical role of the use of such sentences is fairly ambiguous. On one hand the purpose behind the use of such sentences can seem to be to whip up a certain moral fervour, i.e. to *condemn* and *castigate* ('How dare you pass a moral judgement on someone! Shame on you!'). But on the other hand, the point of using such sentences can seem to be rather the opposite, i.e. to lull one into something like moral anaesthesia ('Well, of course you might not care to be a Nazi yourself, but if someone else wants to be a concentration camp commandant and make lampshades of human skin, that's his business. Let's not be judgemental.'). Thus, the purpose behind the employment of sentences like (i)–(iii) often seems somewhat paradoxical. It seems to be to condemn anyone who condemns anyone, to take a firm stand against taking firm stands.

   A large part of the programme of the next few chapters will be to distinguish various things which might be meant by saying that morality is 'subjective' or 'relative', or, more vaguely, by sentences such as (i)–(iii). Sometimes such sentences are employed meaninglessly or in ways that involve conceptual confusion. Sometimes what is said is just self-contradictory. Again, sometimes what is meant is something true, but trivial, uncontroversial, or hardly worth saying. But what is meant on other occasions by calling morality 'subjective' or 'relative' turns out to be something interesting and very controversial. In that event we will want to see whether any of the meta-ethical views we have discussed entail or commit one to 'subjectivism' or 'relativism' in any of these clear, interesting, and controversial senses. Finally, we will want to see whether either 'relativism' or 'subjectivism' (in their interesting senses) makes for any *practical* difference at the level of everyday decision-making.

META-ETHICAL SUBJECTIVISM

There is at least one clear sense of 'subjectivism' worth discussing. As a preliminary, we will explain what it is for a particular judgement (whether moral or otherwise) to be subjective. This explanation involves the notion of a disagreement or a dispute about a judgement:

D1 Judgement j is subjective *iff* the proposition that one person claims (or thinks) that j while another 'disagrees' (as we say) with him (denying j) *does not entail* that some party to this dispute is mistaken. ['Iff' is short for 'if, and only if'.]

Hence, a certain matter is a subjective one if the mere fact that there is a dispute about the matter does *not* make it *necessary* that either side is mistaken.

On the other hand, if a judgement is not subjective, it is objective:

D2 Judgement j is objective *iff* the proposition that one person claims (or thinks) that j while another 'disagrees' (as we say) with him (denying j) *does entail* that some party to this dispute is mistaken.

Where a matter is an objective one, the mere fact that there is a dispute about the matter makes it *necessary* that someone is mistaken. For example, suppose P says 'That is wrong' about something and Q says 'That isn't wrong' about the very same thing, in the very same circumstances, etc. The dispute here will be about a subjective matter provided it still could be the case that neither P nor Q is mistaken. But if someone must be mistaken, the dispute is over an objective matter.

More generally, *meta-ethical subjectivism* holds that *all* moral judgements are subjective (in sense D1); a particular meta-ethical theory is subjectivist if it entails this. By contrast, *meta-ethical objectivism* holds that *some* moral judgements are objective (in sense D2); a particular meta-ethical theory is objectivist if it entails that this is so. Notice, by the way, that meta-ethical subjectivism is not an epistemological claim (a claim about what we *know*, or *can know*). Meta-ethical subjectivism is not merely saying that *we cannot know* which side of a moral dispute is the mistaken one, it asserts that the nature of the dispute is such that neither party need be mistaken.

What kinds of meta-ethical views count as subjectivist? Well, clearly *all* non-cognitivist views (including emotivism) are subject-ivist in this sense. According to the non-cognitivist, moral judge-ments are not statements, they are not (even false!) claims of fact. They are not the sort of thing to be either true *or false*. Conse-quently in a moral dispute neither party says anything which has any chance of being 'mistaken'.

On the other hand *most* cognitivists will be objectivists. For a non-naturalist (e.g. Moore) the presence or absence of the appro-priate non-natural moral property is an objective matter of fact. In a dispute someone has got it wrong. Likewise for a naturalist the presence or absence of the natural properties with which he identifies goodness (e.g. being evolutionarily more advanced, or being approved by the majority) will normally be an objective matter. (In a moral dispute someone will know more biology, or have done his opinion polls more carefully.)

However, a certain kind of naturalist will turn out to be a subjectivist. An example: the naturalistic view that 'A is wrong' just means 'I disapprove of A'. Such a view might *look* objectivist because, after all, it would turn my judgement 'A is wrong' into a claim of psychological fact about myself. However, notice that if I say 'A is wrong' and you say 'A is not wrong', we are, by this present naturalistic account, talking about entirely different things (my state of mind and your state of mind, respectively). Each is talking about his own reactions to A. Neither *need* be saying anything false or mistaken. Thus, this naturalistic account does not rule out the possibility that both could be saying some-thing true about themselves. Consequently at least one version of naturalism (and thus of cognitivism) counts as meta-ethical subjectivism.

DESCRIPTIVE RELATIVISM

Let us now consider relativism. We should first note that the sentence 'Morality is relative' (full stop) is not well formed. In that respect it is like 'Jones is taller than' or 'Sydney is north of', which are simply not complete sentences. Anyone who utters 'Morality is relative' states nothing at all unless he can go on to specify *to what* morality is relative. Here are some common further specifications:

(a) to individuals,

(b) to cultures,

(c) to one's special circumstances or 'situation',

(d) to one's beliefs,

(e) to one's commitments,

(f) to the beliefs of the culture one is in,

(g) to the stage of socio-economic development,

(h) to the interests of the ruling class; and so on.

Now one fairly clear sort of 'relativism' makes claims, not about what really is right and wrong, but only about *beliefs* about right and wrong. This version of relativism, usually called 'descriptive relativism', merely claims that, as a matter of empirical fact, beliefs about moral matters differ. Thus when some people say that morality is 'relative' (a) *to the individual*, they are only making the descriptive relativist claim that, in fact, different individuals have differing moral beliefs. Again, when other people say that morality is 'relative' (b) *to cultures or societies*, they only mean to claim that differing moral beliefs are found in different cultures. Indeed a sentence we mentioned earlier in this chapter:

(i) 'What is wrong-for-you might be right-for-me.'

is sometimes used only as a (very misleading!) way of saying that it can happen that you *believe* something to be wrong while I believe that something to be right. Such a claim is hardly controversial. (If only those using this sentence didn't try to mean something much more obscure as well!)

Now of course it is an empirical matter (for anthropologists, historians, psychologists, etc. to determine) just how much difference in beliefs about moral matters there is. However, it is worth pointing out that sometimes what appears to be a difference in moral beliefs really rests on a difference in beliefs about straightforward, non-moral, factual matters. Here is a trite example. An Elizabethan physician might have sincerely believed that he had a moral duty to use leeches to bleed his patients in certain circumstances, reasoning thus:

(1) Physicians have a moral duty to heal and not harm their patients.

(2) In circumstances C, applying leeches is necessary for a cure.

Therefore

(3) A physician has a moral duty to apply leeches to his patients in circumstances C.

A modern physician might disagree with this moral conclusion, reasoning thus:

(1) Physicians have a moral duty to heal and not harm their patients.
(2') In circumstances C (and, indeed, virtually all the time) applying leeches harms a patient.

Therefore

(3') A physician has a moral duty *not* to apply leeches to his patients in circumstances C (or, indeed, in any circumstances).

If we looked only at the respective conclusions, (3) and (3'), we might think there was some great difference in moral values between the Elizabethans and us. However, in our example the difference in conclusion really only rests on a difference in beliefs about causal or scientific matters, i.e. the claims in (2) and (2'). Actually, both views share the same moral major premiss, (1). The point is that one needs to be very careful in assessing the empirical evidence for descriptive relativism. It is actually a lot more difficult to demonstrate difference in *fundamental* moral beliefs than one might first think. Nevertheless, there still is a lot of impressive evidence for such differences. (See Ruth Benedict 1932; Adkins 1960, and much contemporary anthropological work.)

DESCRIPTIVE RELATIVISM AND META-ETHICAL SUBJECTIVISM

We now have one clear sense of 'subjectivism' and one fairly clear sense of 'relativism'. Is there any simple connection between these two theses? The short answer seems to be 'No'.

First, accepting meta-ethical subjectivism does not require supposing that there are all the *actual* differences in moral beliefs claimed by descriptive relativism. Even if, to take emotivism as our example of subjectivism, moral judgements were just expressions of attitudes, so that there is no such thing as a false moral judgement, it is still possible that we all just happen to have the same fundamental attitudes, more or less. (Indeed this could be less than accidental, if there were some socio-biological or sociological explanation of this universal agreement.) Thus it is possible for meta-ethical subjectivism to be true and yet descriptive relativism be false.

Second, and more importantly, descriptive relativism does not entail meta-ethical subjectivism. The fact that different cultures (or even different individuals) have different moral beliefs does not *by itself* show that moral judgements are not objective. The contrary supposition that this does follow would seem to rest on nothing more than the following fallacious argument form:

(1) There is an actual disagreement about some claim j.

Therefore

(2) j is not objective.

If this *were* a valid form of argument, it could be used to show that a lot more than moral judgements are not objective. It could be used to show that practically every sort of judgement is not objective. Even claims about scientific matters would fare no better than moral judgements, for many cultures have not held our current scientific beliefs. But in any case, the above argument form is clearly fallacious. Disagreement about a matter (even a moral matter) is quite consistent with (i.e. does not by itself rule out) one side's simply being mistaken. Disagreement does not demonstrate subjectivity (perhaps it only suggests the matter is rather difficult).

Sometimes the claim of the descriptive relativist is more than that moral beliefs actually differ. Sometimes there is a further claim about the *causal origins* (the genesis) of moral beliefs, e.g. that moral beliefs are causally influenced (or even, completely determined!) by culture, upbringing, interests of the ruling class, or whatever. Thus differences in moral beliefs may be actually *explained* by differences in culture, upbringing, or whatever. However, even if this stronger version of descriptive relativism is true we cannot infer from it alone to meta-ethical subjectivism. To suppose that we can looks very much like a case of what some philosophers call the 'genetic fallacy'.

The *genetic fallacy* (now in a different sense from that described in chapter 4) might be described as the mistake of never bothering to distinguish questions of the *causal genesis* (or origins) of someone's believing a proposition from questions of what evidence, arguments, or justification there may be for the proposition itself. For example, the fact that many people in our society have certain beliefs (e.g. beliefs that Einstein's laws or the Pythagorean theorem are true) might sometimes be *genetically* (i.e. causally) *explained* in terms of cultural upbringing, socialization, toilet-training, charismatic role models, or just heavy-handed classroom indoctrination. But whether or not any of this is so has nothing to do with the question of whether the propositions themselves are true and what justification (e.g. evidence, proofs) they may have. Certainly the existence of such genetic explanations of why some people have the mathematical and scientific beliefs they do does not demonstrate that the propositions themselves are not about objective matters.

I suppose we normally think that *one* possible genetic explanation of why a person has the belief he does is just that he is acquainted with and has appreciated all the evidence and good arguments (i.e. justification) there are for the proposition and has then reasonably concluded it is true. But, possibly, the claim a descriptive relativist wants to make is that (even if this occurs in regard to other kinds of beliefs) this is never the correct genetic explanation of our having the moral beliefs we do. The genetic explanation of our having moral beliefs always gets back to purely irrational (or non-rational) roots (e.g. toilet-training or whatever). Now it would be rather amazing if this were true. At first glance (and even second or third), a few people, at least, appear to make some real attempt at impartiality, consistency, rationality, in forming their considered moral beliefs (e.g. conscientiously trying to discount the prejudices of their own particular backgrounds). It would require rather special counter-evidence to show that these appearances are in fact illusory.

But even if a descriptive relativist has the evidence in hand to show that all our moral beliefs have completely irrational roots, this would at most lead to *epistemological* scepticism about moral beliefs, *not* to any conclusions about the *subjectivity* of morals. At most it would show that we poor humans can never achieve *knowledge* (i.e. something involving *rationally* founded beliefs). But this would not rule out that we might occasionally believe (on irrational grounds) what is true (i.e. we might sometimes happen upon *true belief* in moral matters). Nor would it show that in a moral dispute neither side is mistaken. The defect might be *in us*, not in morality.

CONCLUDING REMARKS

I have argued that no ordinary form of descriptive relativism *just by itself* entails meta-ethical subjectivism. Of course it is still possible that some version or other of descriptive relativism might be one premiss in a *larger* argument designed to demonstrate meta-ethical subjectivism. But then we need to ask ourselves what these additional premisses might be. I invite you to try to do just this.

I also argued, more particularly, that no claim about the genetic origins of our moral beliefs *by itself* demonstrates that morality is meta-ethically subjective. But possibly this claim could be put into the context of some larger argument (with additional premisses) designed to show something like subjectivism. Again, I invite you to think more about this.

QUESTIONS

1 How does meta-ethical subjectivism differ from the subjectivist ethical theories discussed in chapter 2?
2 In chapter 7 one version of descriptive relativism was employed against non-naturalism. Does the discussion in the present chapter show that this move was mistaken?
3 Is the genetic fallacy really a fallacy?

FURTHER READING

Sound introductions to the issues discussed here are Brandt (1959: ch. 5) and Hospers (1961: 34–6). Edel and Edel (1959) present and reflect on ethnographic data, while Benedict (1932) is a whole-hearted relativist. Duncker (1939) argues that the appearance of moral diversity is misleading, covering a deeper unity, and is criticized in Snare (1980).

Freud's account is presented in (1913; 1930). Aronfreed (1968) gives a more contemporary and measured account of internalization, while Scott (1971) emphasizes its sociological dimension. Piaget (1948) and Kohlberg (1969) present genetic accounts of the development of a mature moral consciousness. Wilson (1975) gives the classic exposition of socio-biological approaches to the origins and nature of morality. Richards (1971) gives a sophisticated and important discussion of the issues and problems genetic accounts face. (Chapter 9 also deals with the issues genetic accounts raise.)

9

Genetic accounts which debunk morality

Nietzsche, Freud, and Marx are the three great modern debunkers of morality. While their theories differ in quite fundamental respects, they are alike in two respects. First, each offers an account of the origins of, or an explanation of, our having the moral beliefs we do. Second, the account given in each case suggests that in making moral judgements and taking them at face value we deceive ourselves or become subject to quite basic illusions. According to them, making moral judgements involves a serious misunderstanding of the world or of ourselves. All three give accounts which have seemed to many to undermine, or pose a critique of, moral notions. In this chapter I will give brief sketches of views attributed to Nietzsche and Marx. I will not discuss Freud. In some respects Freud's account belongs to the same general class of explanation as Nietzsche's. It is an explanation in terms of psychological mechanisms. Indeed, some of Freud's mechanisms, e.g. sublimation, are found earlier in Nietzsche. By contrast, Marx does not give an explanation of moral belief in terms of (self-contained) psychological factors, but in terms of social and economic factors. Hence a discussion of Nietzsche and Marx will represent some of the diversity in the genetic accounts given of moral beliefs.

NIETZSCHE'S ACCOUNT OF 'MASTER MORALITY'

Nietzsche, in the first essay of the *Genealogy of Morals* (1967), gives a psychological account of the origins of what he calls 'slave morality'. This term covers a very wide range of value systems, indeed it would seem to cover most of the influential moral systems in western thought, e.g. Stoicism, many strands of Christianity, Kantian ethics, many socialist views, universalist humanitarian values, and also most of the ethical theories we have discussed in any detail. And while it might be a bit ethnocentric, there is some plausibility in supposing Nietzsche meant 'slave morality' to cover anything we might normally call a morality or a normative ethics.

Nietzsche's psychological thesis is that 'slave morality' arises in certain ways as a psychological reaction to a (psychologically) prior value system, 'master morality'. And so Nietzsche's theory of slave morality cannot be given without first discussing his account of master morality. Nietzsche's discussion of master morality is of interest to us for at least two reasons. First, it is of relevance to the discussion of this chapter as a necessary part of Nietzsche's account of the psychological origins of slave morality, and thus of the way in which Nietzsche seems to debunk morality. But, second, Nietzsche's description of master morality is also of interest just as a description of a radically different set of social values which, by contrast with ones we are more familiar with, sets our own into more relief. For our discussion of descriptive relativism (in chapters 8 and 10), it provides a rather striking example of what a rather different set of social values would be like. At least it contrasts sharply with the Stoic-Christian-Kantian-humanitarian tradition. It gives us a better grasp of the wide diversity there might be in values.

In line with this second interest, I propose to illustrate Nietzsche's notion of a 'master morality' by a particular historical example: the aristocratic code of values that seems to be reflected in Homer's epics (an example Nietzsche himself uses). Here I follow Adkin's (1960) description of the ancient Greek aristocratic values of those to whom Homer's poems were originally directed (rather than those they were about). Possibly these were not the values of the whole society but only of an upper class. Even so, the lower classes could not have easily escaped being influenced by the valuations of the dominant class.

(a) The highest valued sort of person

Master morality is concerned in the first instance with the assessment of persons, rather than with principles of right and wrong choice. It is a virtue morality. Like slave morality, master morality evaluates persons along a spectrum of evaluation. There is a highest valued sort of person and a lowest valued sort of person. For the

Homeric Greeks the highest valued sort of person was the *agathos*, the *aristos*, the *esthlos* (i.e. roughly, the noble man, the best kind of man). Later Greeks spoke of the *kalokagathos* (the gentleman). In the Homeric value system, the *agathos* had qualities ('virtues') such as the following, which stress superiority in the arts of war: strength, physical courage, cleverness or wisdom in devising strategy, skills in the arts of political persuasion, excellence of birth and body. That the values here are sexist and military is perhaps rather incidental. What is essential to its being a master morality is that these virtues are a matter of actual achievements, actual successes, actual abilities and skills, actual excellences. Different master moralities will list different kinds of success, abilities, excellences. What also seems essential to a master morality is that a 'shame standard' of evaluation be central (rather than a 'guilt' or 'sin' standard). In Homeric values the appeal comes very close to something like an aesthetic standard of evaluation rather than to what we, in our cultural context, would recognize as a moral standard. In all that he does, the most highly valued person under Homeric values, *agathos*, is *kalos*, i.e. fine, elegant. His actions, his movements, his life are evaluated in terms that we might find more appropriate to a vase or an athlete. The contrast here is with his opposite sort: the crass, the deformed, the embarrassing sort of person.

A consequence of the application of this aesthetic shame standard, with its emphasis on actual abilities and successes, is that the notions of 'intention', 'motive', and 'will' play a very different, and somewhat lesser, role than is the case in our value system. Of course the intentions of the agent assessed can be relevant even under Homeric values, but in a different way. In so far as an actual history of successes (say, in battles) counts, it will do little good for the agent to point out that he was trying to win. Of course, in regard to determining an agent's skills and abilities, intention can be relevant, even if in subsidiary ways. If the agent wasn't, on a given occasion, really aiming his weapon at a certain mark, the fact that it was very wide of that mark will not be evidence of his lack of skill. And, furthermore, no doubt the presence of certain motivations (e.g. pugnacity, endurance, resolve) will be very relevant to the evaluation of the agent as an *agathos*. But beyond these ways in which will, intention, and motive are relevant to evaluation, there isn't much scope for the language of excuse, for saying things like, 'But I didn't mean to . . .', or 'I acted under duress', or 'My will was causally determined', or 'Society made me this way'. If an apple is rotten, going into the causal history of how that came about will not make it any less rotten. No Homeric Greek ever *intended* to be low-born, ugly, inept, or to trip over and fall on his face. But his pointing that out can hardly be expected to make him look less silly, any less of a failure or an embarrassment. Indeed it could only bring more attention to bear on his best-forgotten shame. Shame is very often a matter of defeat, birth, or some other ill-fortune over which he has no control. Hence, the language of 'responsibility', 'blame', and 'excuse', so important in our moral and legal universe, rings distinctly hollow by Homeric standards. In the *Odyssey*, when Homer speaks of the 'shameful' behaviour of the suitors towards Odysseus' household, Homer does not mean, as we expect, that the suitors' behaviour is shameful *to them*. He means it as an insult and a shame *for Odysseus* (Adkins 1960: 41). But of course Odysseus was, up to that time and to his shame, powerless to stop them. The issue was not one of 'fault', 'responsibility', or 'excuse', but of keeping face.

Another consequence of the application of the shame standard of evaluation is a greater emphasis on the *person-relative* language of pride, face, and revenge, rather than the *person-neutral* language of guilt, sin, and justice. Under Homeric values one person may wrong another (who in turn might seek revenge). But this is not quite yet the notion of doing wrong (full stop). The *agathos* may think that he does right to oppose and try to subdue another while conceding that the other acts best to oppose him and that it would be shameful for that other not to oppose him. However, when thinking in terms of the *person-neutral* language of justice and morality, we suppose that if one person is doing what is morally right in regard to another, it is wrong for the other to impede him. Because the dictates of a shame morality can be person-relative, this value system can actually foster conflict between those adhering to it. And this relates to a third consequence. The *agathos* does not contend with his opposite, the 'bad' (inferior) man, he contends with his like, another *agathos*. Nor does he regard those with whom he contends as 'evil'. In this value system the good fight the good. There is no battle of the 'white hats' against the 'black hats'. Indeed he respects those other 'good men' with whom he contends, for it would be demeaning for him to have to contend with those not of his class (Nietzsche 1967: 1st essay, §10). Serious competition is a sign of estimation.

Typically this shame standard will involve something like a code of honour. This can sometimes make it look as if the *agathos* is acting from a sense of morality or of justice. But, while superficially similar, a code of honour differs from a moral code. Certain things will be just too petty for the *agathos*, e.g. petty squabbles over small amounts of money. The noble is liberal with his money. Again, it may be a point of honour for him to keep his word when he has put his reputation on the line (Nietzsche 1967: 2nd essay, §2). Hence some notions of justice may find a place, but a rather subsidiary place, within a code of honour.

(b) The lowest valued sort of person

In the Homeric system of evaluation the opposite of the *agathos* is the *kakos*, the 'base', 'the wretch', 'the no-hoper'. The characteristics (i.e. defects or 'vices') of such a person are: humility, meekness, long-suffering, poverty, insignificance, cowardice, disease, stupidity. It is the typical person of the very lowest class in Homeric society. (They are not called 'blessed' nor are they said to 'inherit the earth'.) Notice that the attribution of the negative label '*kakos*' does not suppose that particular intentions, motives, acts of will, or a *mens rea* are a condition of being so evaluated. Typically one is a *kakos* (a failure or wretch) by accident, circumstances, defeat, ill-fortune, bad birth, or other defect. Of course no one wants to be *kakos* (just as no one wants to be ugly). It is not a question of whether being *kakos* is voluntary or not. Saying one didn't mean to be *kakos* will not make one less so. In this regard we might note this difference between Homeric values and our values. In Homeric society calling one 'deprived' or even 'socially deprived' would in no way alter one's evaluation as *kakos*. Indeed it would be a way of making the point that *kakos* is precisely what one was. It could not work as an excuse or a ground for compensation, much less as a reproach to anyone else. Likewise to call yourself oppressed, besides being a shameful thing for you to do, might flatter your oppressor, but would not make him feel guilty.

The *kakos*, the wretch, is not the object of moral indignation. He is not evil or immoral. He is, rather, the object of contempt. He is thought unfortunate, loathsome, low class, etc., but not guilty, evil, or sinful. In master morality the notion of the good man, the *agathos*, is the primary notion. The notion of the inferior man, the *kakos*, is a secondary and negative notion. The *kakos* is defined negatively in terms of failure to reach the standard of the *agathos*. He is the failure, not the evil person. Indeed the notion of evil plays no role in this scale of evaluation (see Adkins 1960: ch. 5 on 'pollution'). It is a good/bad (or success/failure) morality rather than a good/evil morality.

NIETZSCHE'S ACCOUNT OF 'SLAVE MORALITY'

In some respects slave morality is just the inversion of the scale of evaluation of master morality. The characteristics of the highest valued person under master morality become precisely the characteristics of the lowest valued person under slave morality, and vice versa. Under the slave morality system of values, humility, meekness, poverty actually become virtues (see St Augustine, Jesus, St Francis). And while these become admirable, pride, contempt for inferiors, and 'elitism' become the prime evils (Nietzsche 1967: 1st essay, §7). However, the inversion (or 'radical revaluation' of values) is rather more complicated than this and involves two further features:

(a) The central role of intention and will

Under slave morality actual success (physical or social), actual abilities and skills (e.g. physical or intellectual), become irrelevant to evaluation. Instead, what becomes crucial is the agent's intentions, his will, his motives. For example, Epictetus the Stoic tells us to disregard those things not in our power (just about everything) and worry only about what is, viz. our own will or intentions. Or consider Kant's claim that the only thing morally good without qualification in a person is a morally good will. In contrast to master morality, slave morality emphasizes questions of responsibility and guilt. Excuses become important. Actual success is not important but intentions are. Consequently, for this value system, but not others, the metaphysical question of freedom of the will becomes of central importance. Whereas in master morality the kind of freedom that is important is a matter of having the strength and abilities that will lead to the overcoming of barriers to actual success, in slave morality that kind of freedom is unimportant, and what is important instead is not whether you win or lose but whether your intentions and motives were good ones (Nietzsche 1967: 1st essay, §13).

Consequently, the lowest valued person under slave morality is not the bad person (the failure or wretch), but the *evil* person. He is evaluated negatively precisely on account of his intentions and motives (e.g. pride, contempt). By contrast, the good person (i.e. *morally* good person) is positively valued because of his good intentions and motives, his sincerity, or his lack of evil motives. In any case his actual achievements or abilities are irrelevant. Slave morality is a good/evil morality rather than a good/bad morality. Furthermore, Nietzsche suggests, while in master morality the notion of 'good' is the basic notion, 'bad' being defined in terms of it, in slave morality the reverse is true. Here 'evil' is the basic notion and the notion of 'good' is more likely to be a matter of avoiding or overcoming those intentions and motives which are evil.

(b) Use of the impartial language of justice and fairness

Slave morality uses the language of justice in its own particular way. It represents its judgements as somehow impartial, making a claim to lack of bias. (Nietzsche also gives a different account of how a notion of justice arises within master morality, which makes no such claims to impartiality. See Nietzsche 1967: 2nd essay, §11.) For example, just punishment claims to be quite other than personal revenge or even a just way of handling the thirst for revenge. Moral indignation represents itself not as personal dislike or hatred, but as hatred of moral evil as such. Again, moral blame represents itself as something other than dislike or striking back at insult. Nor is guilt just personal shame or regret. In its use of the language of morality, slave morality uses language that makes pretensions to person-neutral judgements. The evil or injustice done is not just a matter of one person injuring or wronging another, but of committing a wrong (full stop). It calls for indignation on the part of all morally aware persons, not just revenge on the part of the particular person injured or insulted. Again, while the use of 'good' within master morality tends to be person-relative (good for one person but perhaps not for another), the use of 'good' within slave morality tends to be person-neutral. Some things are just morally good (full stop). In summary, there is more of a tendency for the judgements of slave morality to presuppose or claim some impersonal or impartial stand-point than is the case in master morality. Slave morality is more ready to speak the language of justice and fairness at the deepest level of concern.

THE PSYCHOLOGICAL ORIGINS OF SLAVE MORALITY

So far we have only distinguished, in somewhat idealized fashion, two kinds of value systems. Of course actual societies do not differ in having only the one or the other in pure form. In our own society we are familiar with both, even if within different contexts. For instance, something closer to master morality evaluations are what we use in evaluating football players as either 'good' or 'bad' (e.g. when a coach is trying to decide on new team members). In such a context for a player to plead 'But I never really mean to miss the ball and fall on my face' is more pitiful than mitigating. But even if we can identify some master morality and some slave morality elements in practically all cultures, different cultures still seem to be radically different in just where these elements occur and their order of importance. In some societies master morality values tend to be the 'trump' values while in others slave morality values are the most important values. In Western society (much influenced by Stoicism, main streams of Christianity, Kant, humanism, etc.) there is a strong tendency for slave morality values to trump master morality values. It is considered a moral platitude that to be a (morally) good person is more important than to be a good football player. Even those who mock that assumption tend thereby to pay tribute to the fact that it is the conventionally accepted ordering. Of course it is possible that I am speaking here of only a certain tradition in our society. Possibly this varies somewhat from subgroup to subgroup or even from class to class in our society. But slave morality still tends to be the dominant system of values. On the other hand, in Homeric values the ordering is just the reverse. While talk of justice (*dike*) has a bit of a role, it is a very subsidiary role (having something to do with Zeus). Such evaluations easily get trumped by master morality evaluations. Being called unjust was possibly some sort of reproach, but could not really detract from the high positive evaluation of the successful, highborn *agathos* (see Adkins 1960: 37).

However, Nietzsche's psychological theory does not depend on the assertion that absolutely pure cases of master moralities or of slave moralities ever actually occur. They might, but that is another matter. What Nietzsche's theory claims to do is give an account of the origins of slave morality systems of evaluations (whether they appear purely or as elements mixed in with other kinds of evaluative systems). Nietzsche thinks that slave morality arises as a kind of psychological reaction to master morality. While this is sometimes represented as a historical thesis, i.e. that master morality societies came first, it is better represented as a psychological thesis. In the individual, slave morality modes of thought can only arise as a kind of reaction to master morality modes of thought. Master morality is psychologically prior.

Nietzsche's theory is really a 'sour grapes' theory. He holds that those who end up negatively valued under master morality as failures and wretches ('slaves') are driven both by *shame* at their own low position and by *hatred* of those who are highly valued under that scale of values. To feel this, of course, requires that they, the 'slaves', be subjected to, understand, and indeed adopt initially a master morality assessment of themselves and their relative position. Nietzsche uses the word 'resentment' to cover this combination of shame at one's inferiority and hatred toward the superior types who dominate. This resentment is a smouldering force within those frustrated at their own failure. For those thus frustrated, Nietzsche claims, slave morality is a solution to the frustration. It is a form of rationalization on the part of those suffering from resentment. This works in two ways. First, the slave morality inversion of values is a rationalizing, face-saving device. Rather than be subject to the *shame* resulting from the application of the master morality scale, one just inverts the scale so that one comes out positively valued rather than negatively valued. What was a matter of necessity to the slave, the *kakos*, is turned into a virtue: humility, meekness, long-suffering, poverty. Furthermore, by adopting a standard of values which emphasizes intentions, motives, and will, even the lowest can, by his good intentions and humble motives, be assessed positively. The *kakos* under master morality becomes the 'morally good person' under slave morality (Nietzsche 1967: 3rd essay, §14). Conversely, the characteristics of the *agathos* get turned into vices: pride, contempt for inferiors, concern for success, and pride in abilities. Of course the inversion of values is something done subconsciously. It involves a certain self-deception. As with the fable about the sour grapes, the slave convinces himself that what he formerly wanted but could never get is not really admirable. Instead, what he was all along is what is really desirable.

But, second, the revaluation of values is not only a rationalization driven by shame, it is also driven by *hatred* of those who come out superior on the master morality scale (Nietzsche 1967: 1st essay, §10). The slave morality scale of values places the slave's former superior on the low end of the scale. But of course the assessments of slave morality do not represent themselves as just hatred or resentment. Instead the negative judgements are couched in the language of impartiality. Slave morality speaks of 'guilt', 'evil', 'sin', 'just punishment'. It represents itself as proceeding from some impartial point of view, from indignation at evil, rather than just from resentment. Furthermore, rather more is accomplished by this revaluation of values than the mere rationalized expression of hatred, allowing the slave to live with his situation. It actually succeeds in giving the weak power over their former masters. Nietzsche speaks of the 'slave revolt' in morality. The inversion of values is a kind of (subconscious) ploy whereby the weak and inferior actually do succeed in getting power over their former superiors. But this has to involve a certain (not really conscious) hypocrisy, for the slave will always represent his actions in terms of the impartial language of morality rather than just in terms of getting power over a class enemy. The success of the ploy depends precisely on representing itself as something other than what it is. It represents itself always in the impartial language of morality.

In various respects Nietzsche's account is rather more subtle, as well as more complicated, than the above description suggests. I might mention one further twist in Nietzsche's account. As we have seen, his theory makes use of the notion of the psychological mechanism of rationalization of resentment (his 'sour grapes' story). But he also makes use of another notion of a psychological mechanism, what has come to be called 'sublimation'. Nietzsche believed that when a basic drive (the will to power and the desire to hurt are two he mentions) is continually inhibited or frustrated (as in the case of slaves) these drives get redirected toward the agent himself. Nietzsche held that conscience and guilt are to be explained as the result of the sublimation (or redirection upon the self) of basic aggressive drives when they have no other outlet (Nietzsche 1967: 2nd essay, §§15, 16). This account involves a further psychological mechanism different from the 'sour grapes' mechanism first noted.

DOES NIETZSCHE'S ACCOUNT DEBUNK MORALITY?

It doesn't seem quite right to represent Nietzsche's argument as an argument that morality is subjective. There are two reasons for this. First, it seems much too mild to suggest that all that Nietzsche is saying about slave morality is that it is subjective. He is out to debunk morality. He wants to argue that in making moral judgements and feeling moral emotions we deceive ourselves about the true springs of our actions. We are rationalizing and sublimating. We are mistaken and self-deceived in important respects. But, second, another reason it is odd to suppose Nietzsche is out to show morality is subjective is that his argument involves his taking a value stand. Nietzsche himself has values (and, in a sense, a 'morality'). It is precisely from this value viewpoint that he opposes the morality of impartiality and the morality of responsibility (which emphasizes will, intention, motive). He is against egalitarianism, against all that brotherhood-of-man talk, against 'herd' value systems such as socialism and anti-Semitism (which he thinks arise from resentment). In short, he is against all slave moralities, and not just because they involve illusions about one's own psychology, but because he thinks they are stunting and self-destructive. That is not to say he is exactly for master morality either. He's perhaps for a third thing he calls 'self-overcoming' which, to put it a bit crudely, has both the self-affirmation of master morality and the self-control of slave morality. (It should be noted that Nietzsche's attitude toward slave morality is not totally negative, but is as ambiguous as his attitude toward master morality.)

Nietzsche says quite openly that he's discussing a value question, viz. the value of our values (Nietzsche 1967: preface, §§4, 6; 1st essay, §17, note). Furthermore his standard for evaluating value systems seems to depend on his views about human psychology, about human nature and human drives. Slave morality, for example, while its origins are explicable in terms of basic human drives and psychological mechanisms, also is said to involve both self-delusion and self-destruction, as determined by some account of basic drives. But the fact that Nietzsche takes facts about human psychology to bear on the evaluation of systems of value does make him look a bit like an objectivist. He seems to think that certain psychological facts could do something to show Nietzsche correct and his opponents mistaken. Indeed it makes him look a bit like a naturalist in meta-ethics. No doubt it is a mistake to make out Nietzsche to be too much of an objectivist about anything (see Nietzsche 1967: 3rd essay, §12). But at least two things should be clear. First, Nietzsche's psychological story is not intended to debunk all values. It is a debunking of slave moralities in particular. Second, Nietzsche himself has and defends values. But they are second-order values. He is concerned to discuss the value (for humans) of various value systems. At this level he seems to be discussing something not too different from what normative ethical theory does in discussing the non-moral good.

Two questions arise from our sketch of Nietzsche. First, to what extent is his psychological theory true? (It is hardly a foregone conclusion that he is at all right.) But second, and more to our concern, *if* his psychological account were true, *would* that undermine or 'debunk' in some way the morality of impartiality and responsibility? It does seem a bit too easy just to dismiss Nietzsche's account as an instance of the genetic fallacy, just to say that Nietzsche confuses questions of origins of belief with questions of the justification of belief. The issue in this second question will arise again in chapter 12, where we will discuss certain contemporary approaches to moral theory which rather emphasize the notion of 'impartiality'. The reader should ask, in that specific context, whether Nietzsche's account (or some sufficiently similar one) would, if true, undermine such approaches. Or does Nietzsche just commit the genetic fallacy?

MARX'S HISTORICAL MATERIALISM

Marx, like Nietzsche, gives an explanation, or an account of the origins, of our moral beliefs. Unlike Nietzsche, his account is not an (individualistic) psychological one but a socio-economic one. The core of historical materialism depends on a distinction between (a) 'material base' (something like economic structure) and (b) 'superstructure'. Superstructure includes, among many other things, morality, law and legal institutions, religion, political ideologies. It includes everyday moral beliefs and judgements as well as the worked-out moral theories of philosophers.

The 'base' consists of (i) 'productive forces' (e.g. tools, techniques, knowledge used in production) and (ii) 'relations of production'. Interpretations of Marx differ in regard to 'relations of production'. They are variously interpreted as power relations, economic relations, social relations, production organizational relations, or perhaps some combination of these. But it does seem clear that, say, the relations between employer and employee in a capitalist society, such as would determine the command of the latter over the former in production, the productive activity of the latter, the distribution of the product afterwards, etc. are the sort of relations Marx had in mind.

The idea of 'relations of production' is important in Marx's theory for at least two reasons. First, it is crucial in distinguishing between the important different kinds of socio-economic structures ('modes of production') that Marxism wants to distinguish. Differences in base (including relations of production) are what make a feudal society different from a capitalist society, and both different from a communist society. The employer/employee relation (whatever it is exactly) is right at the core of the capitalist mode of production but subsidiary or nonexistent in the feudal mode of production (where lord/serf might be a relation of production). However, second, the notion of 'relations of production' seems to be essential to the Marxist notion of 'class'. Class membership is not determined in the first instance, in Marxist theory, by behavioural criteria (as is frequently the case in non-Marxist theories). Rather it is one's place in the relations of production which is important. Hence the Marxist notion of class requires the prior notion of relations of production.

Historical materialism is a theory which claims to be able to explain the nature of societies and of social change. At the core of the theory is the claim that superstructural phenomena (e.g. morality, law, state, ideology) depend largely upon, and are largely to be explained in terms of, economic base. While there might be some 'feedback', the real source of social change is at the level of the economic base. While it may sometimes seem to us that moral ideas and moral criticism have brought about social change, in fact they are mere superstructural epiphenomena, i.e. mere responses (for the most part) to the real changes going on at the level of the socio-economic base.

There are roughly two interpretations of Marx's claim that base determines superstructure. The cruder version, sometimes called 'technological determinism' holds that social change (and consequent changes in superstructure) is to be explained ultimately in terms of the 'pursuit of more material good through improved technology' (Miller 1984: 171). A more sophisticated version emphasizes the role of classes. Typical of such a version is the explanation of social change in terms of class conflict and of the existence of certain prevailing beliefs and ideologies in terms of the way they serve the interest of the ruling class. Under the cruder sort of version, moral belief and changes in moral beliefs are to be largely explained in terms of technological change and the facilitating of production. In the more sophisticated versions, moral beliefs function to serve the interest of the ruling class. In either version moral beliefs and judgements have a (socio-)economic explanation. Marx, thus, has a genetic account of moral beliefs.

MARX'S ATTITUDE TOWARD MORALITY

It has been frequently noted that Marx's attitude toward morality and justice is ambiguous, indeed paradoxical (Lukes 1985: chs 1–3; Elster 1986: ch. 5). On one hand, Marx often talks as if moral talk and thought is inevitably mere ideology, mystification, something which only serves the interest of the dominant class. Here Marx seems to take a position beyond morality. Indeed his position seems to be more extreme than Nietzsche's. The latter at least openly admits to taking up a *value* question, i.e. the value of our value system. But Marx often seems to regard it *all* as illusion.

On the other hand, Marx often talks as if he is appealing to moral values. *Capital* is not a dry description, it is dripping with irony and indignation. His talk of 'exploitation' goes beyond mere economic analysis and seems to be more like an indictment of capitalism. It suggests the issue is one of justice, or else of freedom, or at least of quality of life. Again, the discussion of 'alienation' in his early writings suggests a concern with human freedom and self-development and an aversion to various forms of stunting domination. Again, his famous dictum 'From each according to his ability, to each according to his needs' rings like a principle of distributive justice. Finally, the commonly expressed Marxist concern to expose 'class oppression' in capitalist society must look like a moral objection. Marxist judgements using words like 'exploitation', 'alienation', 'oppression' function exactly like moral judgements and it is disingenuous to pretend otherwise. (Aren't we 'class oppressors' supposed to feel a bit guilty? Wouldn't Marxists be disconcerted if, like Nietzsche's *agathos*, we took it as praise?) Some contemporary Marxists actually attribute to Marx principles of distributive justice, e.g. principles of need, equality, or of labour contributions. Others attribute, perhaps not views on justice, but moral principles in the wider sense, e.g. principles of emancipation or self-development. Even if Marx tried to deny it, it is very hard for the reader to see no moral judgements or principles in his discussion.

But how can Marxists have it both ways? How is it possible to debunk *all* moral talk as mere illusion and then go on to engage in a moral critique of capitalism in terms of exploitation, alienation and oppression?

Versions of Marxism which don't debunk morality

Marx's historical materialism might have led him quite reasonably to reject many commonly held moral views, and even to reject the utility of engaging in moral discussion, but in ways perfectly consistent with Marx's having moral views and making moral judgements. To reject commonly-held moral views or even the utility of moral discussion is not yet to debunk morality. For example, historical materialism naturally leads to certain tactical objections to engaging in moral discussion with others, viz. that even if one's moral claims are *true*, convincing others of this fact isn't all that important, because:

(1) Real social change does not come about through discussing moral issues, or even changing people's minds. Indeed, real social change never comes about through conscious choices for such change. To get morality right is not enough. The point is to change things, and according to historical material-ism moral discussion isn't what changes things.

But notice that such a tactical objective is quite consistent with there being such a thing as the right moral theory, with there being a just and unjust.

There is another way in which moralizing might be often impractical for the Marxist. It might be that:

(2) Most people in bourgeois society, for example, are so incapsulated in the values of capitalist society that they almost never recognize their own basic assumptions and are quite incapable of understanding an alternative moral viewpoint. Even the words 'rights', 'justice', 'liberty' get (subconsciously) interpreted in terms of an *unquestioned* property-and-contract ideology. They always get capitalist interpretations. Consequently it is almost always hopeless (except perhaps in a philosophy class, if you have time for that) to get people to see their implicit moral assumptions, and to see that their assumptions are really controversial. Hence Marxists waste their time using the vocabulary of morality. Most of these words have already sold out to capitalism.

But notice that this claim, even if true, does not amount to a debunking of morality. On the contrary it points to deeper moral issues and disputes which normally are not recognized because certain basic values commonly go unchallenged.

A further point, sometimes made by Marxists, is that:

(3) Mere concern with 'formal' rights, liberty, or justice overlooks the socio-economic *context*. For example, the right to vote, or to own property and to enter into contract, or to bring an action in a court might not be of much practical consequence in an extremely inegalitarian, class-dominated economic structure.

However, no moralist could have put the point better. Of course such things have to be morally evaluated, not in the abstract, but in their concrete context. Furthermore, it is important to evaluate how total socio-economic systems work out rather than try to evaluate parts of systems in ignorance of how they function in the whole.

While the above three points are objections to the utility of some or of all moral discussion, it may be that the Marxist point is not so much an objection to moral theory as just, itself, a particular moral view. Perhaps it is merely making moral claims of a relativistic sort. Indeed it might only amount to the following platitude:

(4) Many moral issues are pointless to discuss, or do not even arise, until a certain socio-economic level has been achieved. Many moral issues arise only within certain socio-economic contexts. For example, the issue of the justice of child-minding services available at the place of work may be appropriate in advanced industrial societies, but be quite impractical in some developing societies and totally inapplicable in, say, a desert nomadic society.

But clearly we don't need Marxism or historical materialism in order to appreciate this rather simple point.

However, it is possible that the relativistic claim intended by some Marxists is rather stronger than this. Some attribute to Marx a kind of ethical relativism:

(5) Marxist ethical relativism: There actually is a right and wrong but it is always relative to the mode of production.

On this view what *is right* in capitalist society might not be in feudal society, or in the future communist society. Something else *is right* there. This is not mere descriptive relativism. (5) is not to be confused with the uninteresting claim that people in capitalist societies generally have importantly different moral views than those in feudal societies. Rather, it is the claim that there is a right and wrong but it depends on the society you're in. There are no universal moral principles, but in specific contexts there will be a right and wrong, whether or not you know it.

There are several problems about (5). First, it seems odd to try to derive this moral viewpoint (even if it's relativistic) from historical materialism. It's not at all clear how the 'ought' claim in (5) is supposed to follow from the 'is' claim made by historical materialism. But quite apart from how a Marxist can get (5) from historical materialism, there are a number of problems (5) has in its own right. Chapter 10 will discuss some of the problems any kind of ethical relativism will have. However, in addition to that, Marxist ethical relativism has a special difficult consequence of its own. It seems to take the fire out of the Marxist critique of capitalist society. According to (5), when one is within a capitalist society, there really is nothing wrong about, say, exploitation or gross inequality. It's not just that it isn't *believed* wrong, it *really* isn't wrong. Even someone in a socialist society (or a socialist in a capitalist society) must, according to (5), grant that exploitation and inequality are not objectionable *in a capitalist context*. A related problem is that (5) allows no moral cross-comparisons between societies. There is no ground for saying, for example, that socialism is more just than, or in any way morally superior to, capitalist society. It can provide no moral reason at all for anyone to speed up the overthrow of capitalism.

How historical materialism might debunk morality

Possibly historical materialism is meant to show, not the ethical relativism in (5), but something more like subjectivism or moral scepticism. Perhaps Marx's claim is that what follows from historical materialism is that:

(6) There is never any fact in the world corresponding to 'right', 'wrong', 'just', 'unjust' (although there is the fact that people have moral beliefs). Such belief is always *illusion*. Naturally the social fact that we have such beliefs still has to be explained, but in a way that does not entail that they are anything but illusions. Historical materialism attempts to provide just such an explanation. Moral beliefs can be explained in terms of their serving the interest of the ruling class.

For the purposes of our discussion of genetic theses in this chapter, this is the interesting version of Marx. Here a genetic account of moral belief is thought to debunk all of morality. Naturally, this rather provocative interpretation leads to certain difficulties (within Marxism). If such a complete debunking of morality really succeeds, one wonders: (a) How can there be a Marxist *critique* of capitalism? At most it would look as if all Marx is doing is *predicting* the eventual overthrow of capitalism. Also one wonders: (b) What will be the nature of the future communist society? Will it have moral rules? Will it have social rules or norms for the distribution of roles and economic goods? Will these things get distributed in some way? And if so, won't there be moral issues which arise, for example, over fairness in distribution, and equal opportunity in access to roles? And if these questions somehow don't arise, what will such a society possibly be like? Will morality 'wither away' like the state and the law? Debunking morality is decidedly an easier position to take if one doesn't have to address such concrete issues, if one is content to leave such issues to the future, or to the party.

The genetic fallacy again

And there is a final difficulty with this version of Marx. It does seem to make him guilty of the genetic fallacy. A mere genetic account of certain moral beliefs, by itself, will not automatically debunk those moral beliefs. The arguments various philosophers give for their moral theories (e.g. in chapter 12) may actually still be good ones even if they are not the real explanation of why they make the particular moral judgements they do. Philosophers might have had the moral beliefs first and thought of the justifications later. However, it would be wrong to dismiss the relevance of a genetic account too quickly. Possibly a genetic account could be *part* of a larger account which did undermine moral beliefs (see Snare 1984). Here is a plausible analogy. Some philosophers have held, in regard to religious beliefs, that if the best explanation of the world (e.g. current astrophysics, Darwinian evolutionary theory) does not require God anywhere in the explanation ('I have no need of that hypothesis,' as Laplace said), and if, further-more, our having religious beliefs can be better explained in other ways (than supposing God exists), then we have an explanation that debunks religious beliefs. Notice, though, that even at best a genetic account of religious belief is not itself a sufficient ground for refusing to listen to, and take seriously, the traditional argu-ments for the existence of God (e.g. the argument from design). Such arguments have to be countered in other ways (e.g. by recourse to Darwinism), and not by just waving one's hands and saying 'You only believe in God because you were brought up a Catholic (or because of your toilet-training, or whatever)'. Simi-larly, a successful genetic account of how our moral beliefs come about, while probably a *necessary* part of any attempt to debunk morality, does *not* seem to be, by itself, *sufficient*.

(In chapter 12 we will discuss the possibility that the Marxist rejection of morality (or at least of justice) rests on further grounds than those considered in this chapter. It may be that some versions of Marxism reject the language of 'impartiality' and 'fairness' as a sham, not (just) on the basis of some Marxist genetic account of the origins of our moral beliefs, but on grounds having to do with a Marxist account of classes and class conflict. But that is a different argument.)

FURTHER READING

Barnes and Bloom (1982) give an extreme relativist view. The authors deny the distinction between the justification and the causes of a belief. Pashman (1970: 57–62) gives a more measured discussion, while Snare (1984: 215–25) discusses whether a genetic account of morality can be part of the case for moral scepticism.

The crucial text on the master/slave morality distinction is Nietzsche (1967). Kaufmann (1968) gives an accessible survey of Nietzsche's thought, while Adkins (1960) argues along somewhat Nietzschean lines for certain important differences between Homeric and classical Greek values and modern western values. Elster (1982) discusses a psychological mechanism very close to Nietzsche's notion of resentment as it figures in the creation of slave morality, while Pears (1984) and Festinger (1957) discuss issues bearing on the possibility and nature of self-deception generally. Richards (1971: ch. 13) surveys and discusses the relevance of various kinds of accounts of the origins of moral beliefs and feeling; 250–75 discusses, with many references, theories of guilt and shame; Nietzsche is discussed at 261ff.

Marx did not write directly on morals. His most comprehensive remarks are contained in *A Critique of Political Economy*. *A Critique of the Gotha Programme* is useful for his views on justice and distribution, while *On the Jewish Question* contains an attack on the notion of 'rights'. Buchanan (1983) and Cohen (1978) were instrumental in interesting analytic philosophy in Marx's views, while Elster (1986) gives a fine introduction. Lukes (1985) argues that Marx distinguishes between the 'morality of *recht*', or of rights and justice, which is 'ideological', and the 'morality of emancipation', which is not, while Miller (1984) contends that Marx's ultimate evaluative perspective is not a moral one.

10

Descriptive relativism and varieties of normative relativism

The truth of descriptive relativism is a matter for the empirical sciences. By contrast meta-ethical subjectivism is a philosophical thesis. But neither of these is to be confused with any of the common 'relativisms' which actually take some particular moral or value stance. Any of these latter may be described as instances of 'normative relativism' ('normative' because they take some value stance). In this chapter I shall argue that the outstanding instances of normative relativism are not to be confused with, nor derived from, descriptive relativism.

SITUATIONALISM

Sometimes people intend something *normative* when they say:

(1a) What is right *for one person* may not be right *for another*.

That is, the sentence in (1a) is not intended as just a (highly misleading!) way of stating the descriptive relativist's *empirical* claim. Rather, the claim in (1a) is really about what it appears to be about on the face of it, i.e. a claim about what *is right* for some person. Thus, the claim in (1a) is not about what a given person happens to *believe* is right for him. Indeed (1a) allows that the thing which actually *is right* for a person (but not perhaps for some other) may not be what he believes is right for him. Presumably it is right *for him* whether or not he knows it.

Furthermore, the normative claim made in (1a) in no way would commit one to meta-ethical subjectivism. (1a) denies that there is any kind of act which is always right for everyone. But it is willing to speak of particular acts being right for particular persons. And this might, for all (1a) says, still be an objective matter (i.e. if two people disagree, not about whether something *is right* (full stop), but about whether something *is right for person A*, one of the parties to the dispute must be mistaken).

(1a) might be looked at as only a particular instance of another 'relativistic' normative claim of some interest:

(1b) What is right *in one situation* may not be right *in another*.

For it seems plausible to suppose that where a kind of act is right for one person but not for another, this is due to some difference in their circumstances, properties, roles, or characteristics (in short, to their 'situation' in the widest sense).

Now (1b) is not in fact controversial at all. It corresponds very much to ordinary moral thinking. Here are some examples:

(i) South Pole example (courtesy of Brandt): Hiding a person's clothes is, at worst, a bad practical joke *in the tropics*. However, it would be clearly wrong *at the South Pole*.

(ii) Rule of hospitality (courtesy of Stevenson): A duty to provide hospitality for anyone requiring a place to sleep makes sense in nomadic societies, but not in New York City.

(iii) Truth-telling (courtesy of Plato): It might be right in *most circumstances* to tell the truth, but not to a homicidal maniac wondering where the weapons are kept.

While (1a) and (1b) are pretty much ordinary, common-sense moral views, some moral philosophers (variously called 'situationalists' or 'contextualists') seem to try to conclude rather too much from these commonplaces. Actually, 'situationalism' is used to cover a wide range of not always mutually consistent and not always very interesting views. But in so far as situationalists are saying something new, interesting, and provocative, it seems to be the following: While the situationalist finds no problem about making particular moral judgements addressed to particular situations (presumably such judgements are justified and perhaps even objective), he holds that no general formulation (however qualified) in terms of anything like rules or principles can adequately summarize and capture all these individual justified judgements. Thus, for the situationalist, ethical 'theory' cannot consist in a set of rules or principles: instead the situationalist gives us an (infinite!) list of particular moral judgements addressed to particular, non-repeatable cases. The situationalist holds that any *general* formulation of morality (e.g. utilitarianism, or Ross's theory, or Kant's categorical imperative) is inadequate to grasp the particular moral situation.

Now the case for situationalism really comes down to the argument situationalists give *against* the alternative, i.e. any formulation at all of morality in terms of rules (however qualified). And the main argument it gives against 'rule morality', as it calls it, is just the claim that no form of rule morality is consistent with the common-sense claims in (1a) or (1b).

However, this argument clearly fails. Any rule moralist will point out that the very same general rule can apply, or not, to a certain sort of case depending on the exact circumstances. Thus, if 'Thou shalt not kill' is a rule, it will apply to stripping a person of his clothes at the South Pole, but not to stripping a person of his clothes in the tropics. Thus, stripping a person of his clothes is sometimes wrong, but not invariably wrong. It depends on the circumstances. So even the strictest of rule moralists can assent to (1a) and (1b) without fear of contradiction.

But it might be objected that even if the rule moralist does not think stripping a person of his clothes is always wrong, surely he must hold that *some* types of actions (e.g. killing) are always wrong. And certainly there are absolutists who hold that killing is always wrong. However, a rule moralist can take a somewhat more moderate position than absolutism and deny that any type of act (even killing) is *always* wrong.

Like W.D. Ross (see chapter 3), a rule moralist can assert that killing is only prima-facie wrong. Put more generally, a moderate rule moralist says that there is no type of act (be it killing, lying, or whatever) which is always wrong *whatever the circumstances may be*. He only says that various acts of certain general types are prima-facie wrong, i.e. overall wrong unless outweighed by conflicting, stronger prima-facie duties to avoid some other general type of wrong.

Thus the difference between the situationalist and the moderate rule moralist is *not* that the latter cannot accept the commonplaces (1a) and (1b). The moderate rule moralist tries to determine his *overall* duty in a particular case by weighing the various duty-making or wrong-making features which are present in the particular instance. The situationalist, by contrast, does not find even this much rhyme or reason in the making of particular moral judgements. He just makes his claims of various duties in particular cases, denying all the time that any general feature or property in the individual case bears in any way on the determination. Were he to mention some feature as relevant to the rightness or wrongness in the particular case, that feature could occur again in other cases and would presumably hold the same relevance. And this, of course, would be to admit something like prima-facie rules. Instead, the particular moral judgements of the situationalist are a bit mysterious and oracular, and rather too easy to defend, since he never feels he has to mention any property or feature of an act as a part of the *reason* why it is right or wrong.

Well, I shall leave that controversy hanging at this point. It is a matter for ethical theory. Really, the main thing I want to say about the quite uncontroversial (1a) and (1b), as well as the rather more recondite thesis of situationalism, is that descriptive relativism has nothing to do with any of them. Specifically, none of the foregoing follow logically from descriptive relativism. This is not too surprising. After all, they are *about* rather different things. Descriptive relativism is about how *beliefs* differ. But (1a), (1b), and also situationalism are about how what actually *is right* (whether or not believed so by the person in question) differs from circumstance to circumstance or from person to person.

MORAL PRINCIPLES OF TOLERATION

Some anthropologists and sociologists appear to argue from the truth of descriptive relativism to the specific moral conclusion:

(2a) One *ought* to tolerate (or even respect) the moral beliefs and practices of other persons and cultures.

Of course (2a) makes a moral claim. It asserts that it is morally wrong not to tolerate the moral beliefs of others.

As a moral claim (2a) is rather curious. Admittedly many would accept a rather more *restricted* version of (2a). I myself think that we generally ought to tolerate and make allowance for the beliefs of other cultures about manners, etiquette, good form (what might be called 'petty morals'). And sometimes even greater allowances ought to be made. We generally need to respect different forms of social arrangement (e.g. different forms of the family or kinship relations). But (2a) goes far beyond any of this. It claims we ought always to tolerate all the moral beliefs of other cultures. So this means we must also tolerate slavery (and slavers) where that is culturally accepted, or apartheid where that is entrenched. (2a) is not only against our attempting to do anything to work against such practices, it seems to oppose even our speaking out in condemnation. Thus it leaves little place for the moral reformer or critic.

However, this principle has even more serious problems. These arise from the fact that many of the beliefs it requires us to tolerate are themselves intolerant beliefs:

(a) *Impossibility* In some real-life situations it may be impossible to follow this principle. If I tolerate and respect the values dominant in Nazi Germany, it will not be very easy to tolerate and respect the beliefs of those Jews in Germany at the same time. Perhaps I might tactfully decline to throw stones (or even abuse) at Jews when others do. But the Nazi might then protest that I thereby show no respect for *his* beliefs and practices.

(b) *Self-defeatingness* Even if I avoid the impossibility problem (perhaps by being suitably wishy-washy and noncommittal), following (2a) may defeat the aim of a world where mutual tolerance prevails. Because many, indeed most, cultures have a great many intolerant beliefs in regard to other cultures, the end practical result of tolerating all these intolerant beliefs would be a fairly intolerant world. Thus anyone who is really for more mutual toleration in the world will not be for (2a).

Given these problems, a rather more plausible principle of toleration would make certain exceptions in regard to the special case of the intolerant beliefs of other cultures:

(2b) One *ought* to tolerate (and respect) at most the *non-intolerant* beliefs (and practices) of other persons and cultures.

There is another peculiarity of moral principles of toleration such as (2a) or (2b). They are in a certain respect rather 'absolutist'. That is, the duty imposed in (2a), or (2b), is in no way relative to the beliefs or the culture of the person on whom it falls. Principles like (2a) or (2b) do not require that one first believe or accept that there is that duty. Again, the duty to tolerate other cultures itself falls on all cultures whether or not they recognize such a duty. Of course one might try to 'relativize' the principle of toleration further. Consider:

(2c) One has a duty to tolerate the beliefs of other cultures if one's own culture believes there is such a duty, but if (as is more usually the case) it doesn't, then one has no duty to tolerate other cultures.

Does this principle do anything to strike a blow for toleration? 'Not so's you'd notice.' In fact it is only a special instance of the 'principle of conformity' to be discussed in the next section.

However, the main point I wish to make about the various moral principles of toleration is that none of them seems to follow from descriptive relativism alone. The fact that beliefs differ between cultures does not by itself tell us whether we ought to react tolerantly or intolerantly to those different from us. I am not, of course, saying there are no good arguments for some (perhaps suitable modified) principle of toleration. But, given that it is a *moral* principle, it would be best defended and argued for within the context of some ethical theory. Espousing a principle of toleration does not get one out of having to do ethical theory. Exactly the reverse.

Moral principles of conformity

We find some such thing in the maxim 'When in Rome, (one *ought* to) do as the Romans do'. This could be more generally expressed as follows:

(3a) One *ought* to do whatever the culture one is in accepts as conventional or obligatory.

I suppose I accept some such moral principle in regard to *petty* matters (e.g. such as whether to take off one's shoes on entering a house). But few would accept it across the board. What if what the Romans do is send Christians to the lions? Should one cheer (as is the convention)? And what should one be doing when in the Nazi Reich?

Possibly such objections might be overcome by considering (3a) as only one prima-facie moral duty among many others. (One suspects this prima-facie duty gets frequently outweighed by more important duties in the Third Reich case.) Even so, sometimes the principle of conformity is put forward as the one and only principle of morality. This really constitutes a complete ethical theory:

(3b) Ethical relativism: The one and only feature which *makes* an act A morally right for a person P is A's being required by the moral code of the culture P is in.

Of course ethical relativism is taking a moral stand. Indeed it is a full-blown ethical theory. In so far as it takes a stand on what makes acts morally right it is not obviously any less 'objectivist' or 'absolutist' than any alternative ethical theory.

The rather interesting thing about (3b) ethical relativism is that, while it looks as though it makes all duty relative to cultural beliefs and practices, it is still quite 'absolutist' in one respect. It makes a rather big exception of itself. While every other particular duty depends on (is 'relative to') some culture's recognizing that duty in belief or practice, the basic duty to conform to the moral beliefs of the culture one is in is not itself one which derives from *any* culture's accepting it. It is set down as a quite absolute principle. The duty of the person who happens to be in Rome to do as the Romans do does not itself depend on the Romans' (or anyone's) accepting the ethical relativism of (3b). Certainly the Romans didn't accept (3b). Typically they thought that when in, say, Gaul, they should do as a Roman does in a barbarian country. Furthermore, if the duty in (3b) applied to itself, i.e. required social acceptance before it could be a duty, we could be certain that there never would be such a duty. No culture (including our own) has ever accepted the blanket principle in (3b).

So far I have been pointing out several difficulties with (3a) and (3b). However, the main point I wish to make is quite simple. Descriptive relativism by itself constitutes no argument whatsoever for either (3a) or (3b). That different cultures *in fact* have different moral beliefs does not show that we *ought* to conform to the beliefs of the culture we happen to be in.

Relativity to moral beliefs

The following sort of claim certainly looks relativistic:

(4) What is right for a given person (or culture) is (or at least depends on) what that person (or culture) believes is right.

But while such a claim may be relativistic, it still is a moral stand. It admits and declares that specific individuals have specific duties in specific circumstances (depending on what the given individual, and not others, believes). Of course there are several versions of (4). One is a meta-ethical thesis:

(4a) 'A is right for P' $=_{df}$ 'P believes A is right (& C_1 & C_2 &
    ...)'

where 'A' names any act, 'P' names any person, and 'C_1', 'C_2',
etc. give whatever further condition, if any, may be thought necessary by the proposer of the definition.

The main difficulty with any proposal of the form (4a) is that
it suffers from the most obvious defect a definition or analysis
can suffer from. It employs in the definiens the very term or
notion it is trying to define, i.e. 'right'. If one didn't already know
what *being right* was, how would it help to explain it in terms
of *believes right*? One wouldn't know *what* exactly it was that
was being believed when an act was believed right.

A version of (4) which escapes the above difficulties is not a
meta-ethical claim, but an ethical theory:

(4b) The one and only feature which *makes* an act A morally
    right for a person P is (or always involves) P's believing A
    is the morally right thing for him to do.

Notice that, since (4b) is not offered as a definition but only as
a true claim about why acts are right or what makes them right,
it is not quite so obvious that there is something circular or
improper in the use of the second 'right'. (4b) is not trying to
explain the meaning of 'right', but only to say something true
using the notion.

Even so, (4b) is very peculiar. It is subject to a Euthyphro-
difficulty. Let us suppose (4b) were true. In that event it would
be impossible for someone to believe (4b), the true story about
morality, and at the same time have any moral duties based on
(4b), allegedly the only basis of moral duties. The only people
who, on the basis of (4b), might have any moral duties would be
those benighted people who mistakenly base their moral beliefs
on something besides (4b). They would have quite mistaken
grounds for believing something was their duty *and then*, in virtue
of (4b) and quite unbeknownst to them, it would *become* their
duty, although not at all for the reasons they thought. On the
other hand, a more informed person who realized (4b) was the
only basis of morality could not rationally believe any act of his
was right until it met the belief condition specified by (4b) that
he already believe it to be right. However, the rational, informed
believer in (4b) cannot already, independently of (4b), have any

beliefs about what is right. Thus (4b) is a rather odd ethical theory, for it can never be of any practical consequence for any person who believes it and tries to apply it consistently and clear-headedly to his own choices. Thus, we may regard it as only a pseudo-principle of moral choice.

Relativity to acceptance or commitment

An ethics of commitment can avoid some of the worst absurdities of an ethics of belief:

(4c) The one and only feature which *makes* an act A morally right for person P, is (or always involves) P's having accepted (or undertaken or agreed to, or committed himself to) a moral code which requires P to do A.

Here 'to accept' does not mean 'to believe' but something more like 'to promise' or 'to undertake'. Otherwise we get the difficulties of (4b) all over again.

However, the plausibility of (4c) seems to rest on the (itself rather overly moralistic) view that something like a promise is the one (and only) thing which can morally bind a person or create an obligation on him. But this only provokes us to ask, 'But why is it that one's promises or commitments give rise to moral obligations?' It rather looks as if the obligation to keep one's promises (or commitments, or whatever) is the one big exception to the relativistic claim in (4c). We just ought to keep them, whether or not we've previously agreed to keeping our promises. Thus the proponent of (4c) is something of an absolutist. The alternative seems to be to suppose that even the obligation to keep our promises rests on some actual, temporally prior, second-order promise to keep our first-order promises. But why should *that* promise have been binding? Did we perhaps, prior to that, make a third-order promise to keep our second-order promise to keep our first-order promise? But what made that promise binding? And so on. (Is this a *vicious* infinite regress?)

A confusion

I suspect that (4b) and (4c) *look* more plausible at first sight than they really are simply because they are confused with very different (and somewhat more plausible) claims:

(4b') A person P is not to be *blamed* (or *condemned*) for some morally wrong act A if he believed he was acting rightly or permissibly in doing A.

and the slightly stronger:

(4c') A person P is not to be *blamed* (or *condemned*) for some act A where P has not *accepted* (or *committed himself* to) a moral code which counts his doing A as wrong.

(4c') is slightly more controversial than (4b'). Most people think we are entitled to condemn Nazi atrocities even if (and perhaps especially because) the Nazis involved did not accept the moral code in terms of which they are condemned. (But see G. Harman 1977: chs 8–9.)

However, the point to be made in regard to (4b') and (4c') is that they are judgements having to do, not with right and wrong *action*, but with questions of how *persons* are to be assessed as morally good or bad. (See chapter 3 for the difference between these two kinds of moral judgements.) Thus neither (4b') nor (4c') denies that there can be (an 'absolute' or 'objective') right or wrong action to be chosen. Quite the contrary, they seem to presuppose that sometimes what is chosen is wrong in itself. They merely specify certain 'excusing' conditions (i.e. non-belief or non-acceptance) under which the agent is, nevertheless, not to be blamed or held responsible for his admittedly wrong choice.

Thus (4b') and (4c') make moral claims which are to be properly considered within the context of that area of ethical theory which considers questions of moral blame, responsibility, and so on. But whatever plausibility claims (4b') and (4c') may turn out to have in no way buttresses the case for (4b) or (4c), which are about rather different matters. Indeed, except for this confusion, few would be tempted to assert (4b) or (4c) at all.

CONCLUSIONS: DESCRIPTIVE RELATIVISM AND NORMATIVE RELATIVISM

The 'relativistic' claims (1a) and (1b), as well as the quite distinct claim of situationalism, presuppose that there is a right and wrong which applies to particular circumstances at least. Furthermore, relativistic claims (2a), (2b), (2c), (3a), (3b), (4b), and (4c), not to mention (4b') and (4c'), all make outright moral claims. In each case it can be seen that the particular moral claim (an 'ought') does not follow from the descriptive relativist's 'is' alone. It's hard to see why anyone should have thought the mere empirical fact that moral beliefs differ could by itself be a sufficient reason for accepting any of the particular moral stances discussed in this chapter.

Notice, furthermore, that to think the contrary would be to suppose that an 'ought' (i.e. one of the above 'relativistic' moral claims) could be derived from an 'is' alone (in this case the truth of descriptive relativism). If there were, contrary to our discussion, some such valid argument (say, to the conclusion that we *ought* to be tolerant, or that we *ought* to conform), and if, furthermore, descriptive relativism were true (as it might well be), all the following would be true:

(a) Non-cognitivism would be false. At least one moral claim (that we ought to tolerate, or that we ought to conform) would have been shown to be *true* (or near enough to the same thing).

(b) Hume's gap thesis would have been refuted. There would have been at least one valid derivation of an 'ought' from an 'is'.

(c) Meta-ethical subjectivism would have been shown false. There would be at least one moral claim (that we ought to tolerate, or whatever) such that if anyone disagreed with it he could be shown to be mistaken just on the basis of the empirical truth of descriptive relativism.

However, we have seen no reason to suppose, at least in the particular cases considered, that there is any such derivation from descriptive relativism alone. If there is a moral case for toleration, conformity, belief-dependent duties, commitment-dependent duties, or whatever, it does not seem to rest merely on descriptive relativism.

QUESTIONS

1 Could an ethical theory hold that a person's duty might depend on something other than features of him and his situation? Might two persons with exactly the same characteristics, roles, and properties in exactly the same circumstances nevertheless have differing duties?

2 How does ethical relativism (3b) differ from (3c) meta-ethical relativism: 'Morally right for P' $=_{df}$ 'being required by the moral code of the culture P is in'?

What special problems does (3c) have which (3b) does not?

3 Is this a Euthyphro-like pair?

(i) An act is right for me because I believe it right.
(ii) My beliefs about what acts are right for me are rationally formed, i.e. my beliefs about what acts are right are based on (i) above.

FURTHER READING

Basic discussions of normative and descriptive relativism are Brandt (1959: ch. 11), Cooper (1981), Harrison (1979: 273–90), and Stace (1937: ch. 1). Herskovits (1947: ch. 5) and Westermarck (1932) give the classic anthropological argument for normative relativism. Fishkin (1984; 1980: 85–106) presents empirical evidence for the psychological naturalness of the movement from descriptive to normative relativism, and seeks to establish a 'minimal objectivism'. Taylor (1954: 500–16; 1958: 32–44) opposes too easy an absolutist/relativist debate, and argues that ordinary moral thought has the resources to cut across cultural boundaries, while Wellman (1963: 169–84) is useful for clarifying the various senses in which relativism may be intended. See also Nielsen (1966), Ladd (1973), and Meiland and Krausz (1982).

Much of situational ethics draws on the radically individualist side to Protestantism. The crucial historical source is Kierkegaard (1941), discussed in Warnock (1967: ch. 12). Fletcher (1966) gives characteristic formulations, while, from a different tradition, Prichard (1912) argues that basic moral judgements are particular.

On absolutism and its critics, see Anscombe (1958), Bennett (1966), and Rachels (1970).

11

Whether meta-ethical subjectivism has practical consequences

I argued in chapter 10 that none of the kinds of normative relativism considered there follows from the empirical thesis of descriptive relativism (alone). Now we need to consider whether any kind of normative relativism could be based, instead of on descriptive relativism, on a subjectivist meta-ethics. It might seem plausible on first learning about meta-ethical subjectivism to suppose that it somehow lays a basis for certain normative principles such as toleration, cultural conformity, ethical relativism, liberalism, or the view that what is right is whatever one believes is right, or even the view that 'everything is permissible' (which, as I argued in chapter 1, is also a moral stance).

META-ETHICAL SUBJECTIVISM AND NORMATIVE RELATIVISM

First appearances are deceiving. There is, in fact, a quite knockdown and sweeping argument that meta-ethical subjectivism cannot be any part of a *sound* argument for any normative conclusion whatsoever. In particular, meta-ethical subjectivism cannot be true and at the same time a reason for accepting some version of normative relativism.

Let us try to suppose the opposite. Let us imagine that there was such a sound (i.e. valid with all true premises) argument:

(1) Meta-ethical subjectivism: All moral judgements are subjective.
(2) P_1
(3) P_2

.
.
.

Therefore

(n) [some normative (moral or value) claim]

where P_1, P_2, . . . are the further premisses (if any) necessary to make the argument valid.

Now in a sound argument all the premisses are true. In particular, that means premiss (1), meta-ethical subjectivism, is true. Furthermore, the normative conclusion, (n), is true (because a sound argument is not only valid but has all true premisses). But now we are landed in a contradiction. The demonstrable truth of the conclusion means that at least one normative judgement, viz. (n), is *not* subjective, but is quite objective. Anyone who disagrees with (n) (e.g. recognizes no duty to tolerate, conform, or whatever) *must be mistaken*. But this one instance of an objectively true normative judgement is sufficient to show that meta-ethical subjectivism is false. Thus our supposition of a sound argument requires us to believe both that meta-ethical subjectivism is true and that it is false. The only way to avoid the contradiction is either to suppose that meta-ethical subjectivism is not true to start with, or else accept that, if it is true, its truth cannot be any part of the reason for accepting any value judgement whatsoever. Meta-ethical subjectivism gives us no reason to be tolerant rather than to be intolerant, to be permissive rather than Victorian, to be liberal rather than illiberal, and so on. Actually, there is nothing particularly surprising about our result here. It *is* paradoxical to expect that one could rationally base some particular normative stance precisely on the claim that no normative stance can be rationally based. Meta-ethical subjectivism seems to give us a bleak moral landscape. Its moral and value judgement consequences are nil. And must be.

But now there is an opposite extreme to be avoided. While it is a clear *fallacy* (the term is not too strong) to try to *base* some value claim on meta-ethical subjectivism, it does not follow that a meta-ethical subjectivist cannot *also* take normative stances. There is nothing at all *inconsistent* with holding meta-ethical subjectivism and at the same time holding some particular normative view (e.g. toleration, conformity, or whatever). The fallacy consists only in thinking the two have anything to do with each other. Furthermore, it is just as *consistent* for a meta-ethical subjectivist to take an 'intolerant', 'repressive', 'illiberal', 'Victorian', or 'absolutist' moral stance as it is for him to take any 'relativist' value stance, such as those discussed in chapter 10. Any version of normative relativism must be argued for within the context of ethical theory. It is no less a moral or value stance than any other normative claim. The truth of meta-ethical subjectivism, if it is indeed true, gives no special advantage to the normative relativist.

META-ETHICAL SUBJECTIVISM AND FREEDOM OF CHOICE

It sometimes seems to be suggested (e.g. perhaps by J.-P. Sartre and R.M. Hare) that if something like meta-ethical subjectivism is true, then this strikes a blow for 'freedom'. Even if this suggestion were (in some sense) true, it would not of course constitute an argument for the truth of meta-ethical subjectivism. However, it would suggest that meta-ethical subjectivism has certain practical consequences to do with freedom which meta-ethical objectivism might not. Do subjectivism and objectivism differ in the degree of freedom they afford? That will depend in part on what sort of 'freedom' we are talking about.

(a) Moral principles of social and political freedom

It is sometimes said 'We all have to make our own choices', where this is not intended as an empty or trivial remark on the logic of the word 'choice', but as the significant and practical claim that in some respects we *ought not* to force others, or even criticize others, or perhaps even tell others what to do. Extreme versions of this sort of claim would be:

(5a) We ought not ever to *force* others to do anything (even to do what they ought to do).
(5b) We ought not ever to *criticize* or condemn others (when they have not done what they ought to do).
(5c) We ought not ever to *tell* others to do anything (even when there is a right thing for them to do).

I continue the numbering from the previous chapter inasmuch as the above claims are pretty clearly normative (although not particularly 'relativistic').

(5a), (5b), and (5c) are extreme moral claims which most of us do not really accept. If we really accepted (5a), we could not justify society's having any system of criminal law whatsoever, for such a system, among other things, threatens with punishment those who choose to perpetrate violence against others. Indeed (5a) is rather self-defeating if freedom from coercion is supposed to be the goal. Society's failure to coerce and threaten by law those who would injure and coerce others would probably mean that in practice most of us would be very unfree indeed, for we would be coerced and threatened by those persons society is too squeamish under principle (5a) to threaten or coerce.

Thus (5a) is not to be confused with various versions of *liberalism* in social political philosophy such as:

(5a') In some circumscribed area of life (usually called the 'private sphere'), we ought not to make individuals do what it is right for them to do.

This principle allows that coercion can be permissible and justified in some areas of life (e.g. against a person whose wrong-doing consists in harming others). However, in other areas of life coercion may be morally inappropriate *even against wrong choices*. In the 'private sphere' of life the individual has at least a prima-facie moral right (against the use of coercion by society, the state, or other individuals) to act on his own choices even though some of his choices may be wrong ones. (For the classical exposition and defence of liberalism see Mill 1859.) Of course even (5a') is very controversial.

Also, we could probably formulate rather more plausible principles of social tact and diffidence, (5b') and (5c'), which would be like (5b) and (5c) except that they would allow that some acts (e.g. child-bashing) are so iniquitous that it becomes permissible and right to object or tell people they are doing wrong.

All the above (5)-claims are normative claims. Indeed they seem to be doubly normative. First, they seem to allow that sometimes what persons actually choose to do is *wrong*, but, second, they assert that it is, either always or sometimes, *wrong* for us to interfere in various ways with these (wrong) choices.

All these (doubly) normative principles of freedom are, quite clearly, not to be confused with, or derived from, meta-ethical subjectivism. As we have seen in the previous section, the argument for a normative principle, even of liberty, simply *cannot* involve meta-ethical subjectivism. Meta-ethical subjectivism is *just as consistent* with 'illiberalism', 'authoritarianism', 'paternalism', or whatever, as it is with liberalism. Liberalism gets no special advantage should it turn out that meta-ethical subjectivism is true.

(b) Irrationalist freedom

Some situationalists, most existentialists, and perhaps even some analytic philosophers such as R.M. Hare *seem* to suggest that if morality were (more or less) subjective that would leave us *free* to choose our own moral values. On the other hand, if it should turn out that morality is objective that would leave us unfree in some objectionable way. If, for example, it were possible to give good reasons, evidence, considerations, and arguments for moral judgements, that would somehow be *forcing* or *limiting* people in the moral judgements they could make or the moral beliefs they could have.

Now it is true that good evidence, good reasons, good arguments are somewhat *compelling* (at least for clear-headed people). But it is hardly obvious that this is some sort of objectionable forcing. Consider how odd it would be to say the same sort of thing with regard to non-moral claims (e.g. empirical claims or mathematical claims). Would we say 'If it were possible to give scientific evidence or mathematical proofs for certain propositions, citing this evidence or giving this proof would be using undue force to alter beliefs'? In any case, giving arguments, evidence, or reasons is not quite in the same category as using thumbscrews, blackmail, propaganda, advertising techniques, or brain-washing in order to get agreement. As a matter of fact, it may be that one is likely to be in a position to resist the various forms of belief control and manipulation only to the degree that one has the ability to examine evidence and arguments for oneself.

Furthermore, the subjectivist who says 'One of the advantages of subjectivism is that it avoids an objectionable sort of unfreedom' must be careful that he himself is not slipping back into tacit objectivism. The judgement that a certain kind of unfreedom is objectionable is itself a *value* judgement. And if meta-ethical subjectivism is true, even this judgement about freedom cannot be taken as objective, i.e. it is possible for someone else to hold that such unfreedom is not objectionable without making a mistaken judgement. Similar points may be made in regard to subjectivists who praise their view as somehow 'non-elitist', or 'democratic', or some such thing.

(c) Choosing versus discovering

However, a meta-ethical subjectivist might argue, not that his view has *more valuable* consequences than meta-ethical objectivism, but only that it has *different* consequences. On one hand meta-ethical objectivism offers us the prospect of *discovering* what moral values there are. Meta-ethical subjectivism, on the other hand, offers us the prospect of *choosing* (or inventing, or creating) our own moral values. Let us not worry about the value question of whether choosing is 'nicer' than discovering. Choosing is, at least, different from discovering. This would seem to make for an important practical difference between subjectivism and objectivism.

But before going any further it's worth noting that the notion of 'choosing values' is rather obscure and suspect, not one to be accepted without question. While we have some idea what it is to choose to do particular actions or to choose particular objects, it's not really all that clear what would be meant by 'choosing values'. Of course we *have* values, but it's not clear that we can just turn them on and off as a matter of choice (although the use of that somewhat repellent word 'lifestyle' does suggest it is a matter of this year's flavour). Perhaps we can justify certain values we have in terms of more fundamental ones we have. But even if we can thereupon 'choose' the former, one would think the latter are just values we already *have*. It's not clear what it would be to choose a fundamental value (i.e. where the choice was not based on some prior value one simply *had*). Existentialists some-times seem to talk as if something like this is possible. It would, perhaps, be a 'free' (almost in the sense of 'arbitrary'), existential choice, an act of self-creation. This is a bit mysterious.

But in any case, the meta-ethical subjectivist must suppose *either* that our having ultimate values is something chosen (in some arbitrary, existential manner) *or else* that we have values, not as a result of choice, but, perhaps, as a causal consequence of socializ-ation, biological factors, brain-washing, or whatever. By contrast, the meta-ethical objectivist, while he might allow that all too often our actual moral beliefs result from socialization, etc., holds that there is at least the prospect of discovering the moral facts through the use of reason, arguments, evidence, etc. This is a difference.

EVERYDAY PRACTICAL DIFFERENCES

However, this difference is still fairly 'philosophical'. It's a difference which arises at the fairly sophisticated level of reflection
when one is considering how to, or whether one can, justify the
moral judgements one already makes in everyday life. Subjectivism
says that one can do no more than either just choose some ultimate
values or else refer, without further ado, to whatever values one
already happens to have. Objectivism, by contrast, supposes that
there is something further to discover. But while this difference
is important for the reflective or the philosophical, it's still not
clear that this results in any difference at the level of everyday
moral judgements.

Suppose a meta-ethical subjectivist makes a certain everyday
moral judgement, e.g. the judgement that abortion is wrong in
circumstance C. Let us suppose that there is also a meta-ethical
objectivist who happens to make exactly the same everyday moral
judgement that abortion is wrong in circumstance C. Of course
the two have quite different *meta-ethical* accounts of what it is
to make a moral judgement. But will this *philosophical* difference
come out in any *practical* way if they should happen to make the
same everyday moral judgement? It really isn't clear.

It's tempting to suppose that the subjectivist will have to be a
bit more diffident and circumspect, that he can only venture to
speak *for himself* and *his own actions*, that he won't suppose that
his moral judgements apply to anyone else. We might call this
position 'moral solipsism' (my coinage, not a standard usage). A
moral solipsist does make moral judgements. A solipsist might
say, 'Personally, I think abortion is quite wrong in such and such
circumstances – for me; but that has no implications for what is
right or wrong for anyone else. That's their business.' A moral
solipsist has definite views on what is 'right-for-me' but no views
at all on what is (really) right for anyone else. It should be noted
that moral solipsism is an even more suffocating position than
situationalism. The situationalist is at least as likely to make particular moral judgements about other persons and their particular
acts as he is about his own. The situationalist is against general
rules but not against particular judgements that apply to the acts
of others. Naturally, meta-ethical subjectivism no more supports
moral solipsism than it supports any other moral position. In any
case, if all moral judgements are subjective, one's moral judge-

ments about oneself are in precisely the same bag as one's judgements about others. Subjectivism cannot provide any grounds for discriminating in favour of the former and against the latter.

But in addition to that, there is a real question whether moral solipsism is even a *coherent* moral viewpoint. It seems rather like (to take an analogy from aesthetics) calling your own nose disgustingly ugly in front of a person with an exactly similar nose while denying that your judgement reflects on his nose in any way. That's probably a way to get your nose altered. But perhaps the point can be made in more specific terms. Lloyd Humberstone (1979) points out that two currently influential, even if controversial, theses in meta-ethics would suggest that moral solipsism is not a coherent position. These two theses are universalizability and internalism.

(a) Universalizability

Chapter 5 discussed how a problem for emotivists (and many other non-cognitivists) is to specify how a *moral* attitude is different from other kinds of attitudes and, more generally, how moral value judgements differ from other kinds of value judgements. One way in which non-cognitivists (e.g. R.M. Hare) have tried to mark the distinction is by suggesting that moral value judgements (unlike other kinds of value judgements) have a particular kind of commitment to generality or universality that the other kinds of value judgements may not. Indeed, already in the discussion of Kant in chapter 3, I discussed the view of those philosophers who hold that if a judgement about a particular person is to be a *moral* one, it must presuppose a rule which is to apply to everyone. And indeed there does seem, as the universalizability thesis claims, to be some sort of incoherence in the claim of the person who says, 'Personally, I think abortion is morally wrong. But if anyone else thinks otherwise and wants to have an abortion that's perfectly all right in every respect.' We can understand the claim if it means the person wouldn't *care* to have an abortion herself. But the word 'wrong' is used to say rather more. To think an act wrong is just to deny that, generally, it's all right for others.

There are of course other ways of interpreting this 'personally' claim that make more sense of it. Perhaps the claim is that others who do the wrong thing and have abortions should not always *be blamed* if they sincerely believed it not wrong. There might be a blame principle like (4b') of chapter 10 behind such a claim. Again, perhaps the claim is really that, while it would be wrong for others to have abortions, it would also be wrong to *force* them to do otherwise, or *criticize* them for it, or even just *tell* them that they have done wrong. In short, it might merely be an application of one of those principles of liberty, toleration, or tact discussed at the beginning of this chapter as (5a), (5b), and (5c). But notice that all the ways suggested in this paragraph for interpreting the 'personally' claim do not amount to moral solipsism. On the contrary, they all grant that others do wrong in having abortions. Possibly moral solipsism may seem more coherent a position than it really is because it is so easily confused with mere expressions of liberalism, toleration, tact, or else from a confusion of assessments of the responsibility or blameworthiness of a person for his wrong act with the prior question of whether his choice was indeed for the wrong thing.

(b) Internalism

In chapter 5 the thesis of internalism was mentioned in regard to one of the difficulties which arise for non-naturalism. Internalism holds that to assent *sincerely* to a moral judgement *necessarily* involves having some (even if only slight) motivation of a sort appropriate to the judgement in question and/or having some appropriate feeling, attitude or emotion. Moral beliefs are not just abstract observations about what there is in the world. Hence internalism does seem to have some plausibility. And indeed there is something (conceptually or logically) odd about saying one really thinks something (e.g. slave-trading or drug-dealing) is very wrong while having no motivations or feelings about those who engage in these activities, not even the preference that it not go on.

But now, if internalism is correct, then even the subjectivist who sincerely assents to the moral judgement 'A is wrong' cannot be indifferent to the activities of others. In this respect he will be no different from the objectivist who also sincerely assents to the same judgement.

One practical difference

So far, we have discovered no practical difference between an objectivist and a subjectivist who happen to make the same particular moral judgement. Their differences come out in theoretical philosophical discussions, but not anywhere else. The subjectivist's moral judgements reach out and apply to other persons in just the same way as the objectivist's do.

Humberstone notes that there is perhaps one practical difference. If subjectivism is correct, then, as long as I have a consistent set of moral attitudes and make no empirical or factual mistakes in regard to any of the non-value, subsidiary premisses I employ, then I have no reason for listening to the arguments of others who might be advocating a different position. Of course their views, if they are as careful as I, cannot be said to be mistaken. But, if subjectivism is correct, then neither can mine. If, on the other hand, objectivism is correct, then even if my moral judgements are consistent and empirically informed, I *may* still be missing the truth. Mere consistency in the (ultimate) attitudes or values one chooses, or has, is not enough, according to objectivism. Thus the objectivist may have a reason, which the subjectivist doesn't have, for being interested in the moral arguments of others in favour of opposing moral views. While the subjectivist who makes a moral judgement will admit that opposing (ultimate) moral viewpoints are not mistaken, he will see no point in listening to any arguments for these other (ultimate) viewpoints, because he holds that he too cannot be shown to be mistaken in his (ultimate) moral views.

It is interesting that the one practical difference we can find between objectivism and subjectivism at the level of everyday moral judgements actually shows subjectivism to be the somewhat more conservative standpoint. At least, if subjectivism is correct, status quo (ultimate) moral beliefs never need feel threatened by the opposing moral arguments of the social critic or reformer (provided the status quo values are internally consistent). Nor will a subjectivist ever see much point in listening to such social critics and reformers, much less bothering to change any of his own deep-seated values in accordance with their demands. Traditionally, it has been critics of the status quo who have assumed a kind of meta-ethical objectivism (unless all they were doing was criticizing current practice as failing to live up to the current professed values). It has been much more usual for the defenders of the status quo to rely on the inertia of a smug subjectivism. It seems to be no accident, therefore, that the founder of contemporary meta-ethical subjectivism, David Hume, is also an important source of classical political conservatism. There is much irony in this. Initially it might have seemed that subjectivism has some tendency toward radical, liberal, or permissive values. But this turned out to be a confusion. Indeed, if subjectivism has any tendency at all, it is toward smug conservatism, toward the values of the status quo. 'If all values are subjective, why bother to change?'

There is an important exception to this. It may be that some Marxists are really subjectivists about moral values. They might concede that those who have bourgeois values, rather than proletarian or Marxist ones, cannot be shown to be mistaken. However, they may also think that, while bourgeois or capitalist values are the values of the status quo, nevertheless proletarian or Marxist values are the values that will eventually win out in the class struggle. 'You've got your values. We've got ours. But ours will win out in the end. The future is on our side.' But no claim is made that such values are superior in any objective way. There are some problems with this view. If this alleged victory of proletarian values is too far in the future it may not be clear why anyone with the dominant bourgeois values of the present mode of production should particularly bother to speed up the revolution. This is sometimes called the problem of 'revolutionary motivation'. Furthermore, as the Marxist predictions have come to seem more and more doubtful, the tendency of subjectivism must seem more and more conservative.

However, we should not exaggerate even the one difference we have found at the practical level. Even a subjectivist cannot really be absolutely confident that his values are internally consistent or that the subsidiary empirical premises he employs to get more particular moral conclusions are all that well confirmed. So he will have some reason to listen to what those with opposing views argue. But he will not have quite as much reason as the objectivist.

CONCLUSIONS

Whether meta-ethical objectivism is the case or whether meta-ethical subjectivism is the case is, of course, of interest to those with any sort of philosophical *curiosity* about the nature of the world and what there is in it. But beyond that, it is not at all clear that the difference has all the *practical* consequences that many have thought. Certainly it is not inconsistent for one to assert meta-ethical subjectivism and at the same time make any otherwise coherent moral judgement. Furthermore, when a meta-ethical subjectivist makes a moral judgement it seems to have all the same practical force as one made by a meta-ethical objectivist.

Finally, I shall note in chapter 12 how some of the main methods proposed by philosophers for justifying an ethical theory do not really seem to depend on whether meta-ethical subjectivism or meta-ethical objectivism is true. The same method may be employed whether one thinks of it as discovering or as inventing.

FURTHER READING

Humberstone (1979) and Warnock (1967) give basic discussions of subjectivism. Hare (1952; 1963) and Sartre (1963) suggest that subjectivism is connected with 'freedom', while Mackie (1977) calls on us to 'choose' our values. Williams (1973: chs 2–4) claims to 'defuse' subjectivism.

Mill (1859) is essential for understanding liberalism. Ten (1980) gives a fine critical discussion of Mill, while Wolff (1968: ch. 1) is an uninhibited anti-liberal.

Basic accounts of universalizability are found in Baier (1958) and Hare (1954–5; 1963). Locke (1968) and Mackie (1977) are useful in sorting out the various things that 'universalization' might mean, while MacIntyre (1957) raises doubts about the usefulness and general applicability of the notion.

On internalism, Hare (1952: chs 1, 2) and Hume (1739) provide basic expositions. Frankena (1958) is detailed and difficult, while Snare (1975c) is sceptical of non-cognitivism in so far as it rests on the truth of internalism.

12

Methods of justifying a normative ethical theory

Chapter 3 discussed three particular examples of normative ethical theories (Mill's, Ross's, Kant's). Along the way we also mentioned theistic ethics, subjectivistic ethics, ethical egoisms, situationalism, and ethical relativism. The obvious question which arises is whether there is any rational procedure for deciding between normative ethical theories. How does one (or can one?) justify a particular normative ethics in preference to all the alternative theories? (This is one way to interpret question Q2 which arose in chapter 1.) As you would expect, philosophers disagree about this and have proposed a number of different ways to go about justifying a normative ethics.

Now one might suppose that a philosopher's 'method' would *invariably* depend on his meta-ethical views, in particular whether he held meta-ethical subjectivism or meta-ethical objectivism. Something like this, you might remember from chapter 1, was Socrates' assumption. Socrates seems to have thought that no claims about what acts *are pious* (or *are just*, etc.) could be justified without first determining what *is* piety (or what *is* justice, etc.). Socrates thought one had to begin with meta-ethics. Now this is *sometimes* how moral philosophers have proceeded. For example, Aquinas (*Summa Theologica*, II, Q94, A2) begins with two meta-ethical claims: first, the claim that being good is (=$_{df}$) being sought after, naturally, by all things; second, the allegedly self-evident, analytic truth that good is to be done (i.e. ought to be done). The only further thing Aquinas requires to discover our actual duties is some sort of (empirical or metaphysical) investigation into human nature and natural desires. Thus Aquinas' 'method' for determining our actual duties pretty much follows from his meta-ethical views. An even clearer example is to be found in Spinoza's work *Ethics Demonstrated in the Mathematical Manner*. Spinoza claims to begin with certain allegedly self-evident, necessary axioms, from which a normative ethics is, he claims, ultimately derived. The 'method' according to Spinoza is just to follow his proof.

However, the main methods proposed by twentieth-century philosophers do not seem to depend on whether meta-ethical subjectivism or meta-ethical objectivism is true. At most, the methods receive somewhat different interpretations depending on which is true. If some such method is plausible and defensible, this would suggest, again, that the difference between objectivism and subjectivism is not as important as one might first think. I shall now briefly sketch three methods proposed by philosophers.

1 THE 'DATA' METHOD

Here the appeal is to the (more or less) *particular*, 'common-sense' moral judgements we make in everyday life. It is against such 'data' that the highly *general* formulations of normative ethical theory are to be tested. Thus W.D. Ross (1930: 20n) says:

> To me it seems as self-evident as anything could be, that to make a promise, for instance, is to create a moral claim on us in someone else. Many readers will perhaps say they do not *know* this to be true. If so, I certainly cannot prove it to them; I can only ask them to reflect again, in the hope that they will ultimately agree that they know it to be true. The main moral convictions of the plain man seem to me to be, not opinions which it is necessary for philosophy to prove or disprove, but knowledge from the start . . . .

This makes the 'method' of moral philosophy rather more analogous to the scientific method than to the method of mathematical proof. One does not begin with self-evident axioms or definitions (as in Aquinas or Spinoza), from which particular moral judgements are derived as mere theorems. Instead, ethical 'theories' are put forward, much as scientific hypotheses are, except that they are 'tested' against our everyday, common-sense moral judgements, which here count as the 'data'. For example, suppose that utilitarianism (an ethical 'hypothesis') really does have the consequence that there are occasions when a judge ought to punish a person he knows on the evidence to be innocent, in order to avoid the violence of an angry, bigoted mob, whereas our ordinary, common-sense judgement would consider the judge wrong to do so (or, at least, not obviously right). The 'data' method would take this to be a 'counter-example', or some degree of 'disconfirmation', of utilitarianism. (By contrast, an 'axiomatic' method might regard this as grounds for rejecting the common-sense judgement.)

Now the 'data' method in fact admits of two interpretations, depending on whether meta-ethical objectivism or meta-ethical subjectivism is the case. For an objectivist like Ross, the common-sense moral judgements which serve as confirming or disconfirming 'data' are really to be thought of as perceptions or 'intuitions' of (non-natural) properties or (non-natural) facts. (Ross is sometimes called an 'intuitionist' in meta-ethics.) Ross clearly considers these 'intuitions' to be as much *knowledge* as, say, our ordinary perceptions of natural properties (e.g. that this thing is yellow).

By contrast, a subjectivist interpretation of the present method is also possible. The 'data', i.e. the particular, everyday, common-sense moral judgements, are not regarded as perceptions or knowledge but perhaps only as expressions of our feeling and attitudes. The project is then to come up with an ethical theory which best summarizes or formulates these particular moral judgements. Thus, as before, all our particular moral judgements count as data for or against various proposed general formulations (e.g. utilitarianism). Hume (1777) and Frankena (1973) are perhaps examples of this somewhat more subjectivist interpretation of the data method.

Given the data method (with either interpretation), it is still far from obvious which normative ethics in particular would end up as the most highly confirmed hypothesis (or most adequate formulation). Sidgwick (1874) used the data method to argue for utilitarianism. W.D. Ross, of course, used it in arguing for his deontological set of prima-facie rules. But at least one has some idea how to argue for or against a proposed ethical theory, given this method. I myself suspect that something more like Ross's theory than utilitarianism would result from the use of this method.

2 QUALIFIED 'DATA' METHODS

There are a couple of variations on the previous method. We might consider again the analogy to sense perceptions (say, of colours) as 'data' for hypotheses. Notice that even in the case of, say, confirming or disconfirming the 'hypothesis' that this book is yellow, we do not treat all our colour perception judgements as having equal weight. Some of the 'data' get discounted or thrown out. While the book may look yellow to me on a given occasion, I will not count that perception as all that conclusive if I also know that I have coloured glasses on or that the light is very non-standard or that I have an eye disease. Similarly, some of the moral judgements I make are made in the heat of anger, or in ignorance of the total situation, or are distorted by my own personal stake in the matter, or rest on some misinformation, or simply are the result of some logical mistake in my reasoning. Thus one way of qualifying the 'data' method would be not to count all common-sense everyday judgements equally as 'data', but to count only those judgements made under fairly standard conditions (just as we only count colour judgements made under standard conditions).

However, the phrase 'standard conditions' is ambiguous. It could mean either something like 'statistically frequent' or else something more like 'ideal'. In regard to our colour judgements we hardly need to distinguish these, since they go together anyway. Eye disease is infrequent and viewing things under sunlight is not at all unusual. But things are rather different in regard to moral judgements. To take pains to learn all the relevant facts, to be careful in one's reasoning, to not be swayed by one's own special interests, to attempt to understand what it would be like to be the other person, are all very rarely found in the making of ordinary moral judgements. For example, strong moral judgements condemning homosexuals or persons of other races are not uncommon in some quarters. But it is quite another question whether such statements could be persisted with were the judgements more informed, more consistent, more sensitive to imagination and empathy, more reflective, etc. So it might be appropriate to speak not of 'standard conditions' but of something more like 'ideal conditions', for the conditions may not be fulfilled all that frequently. Thus another modification of the 'data' method would appeal, not to the moral judgements we actually make, but to the judgements we (hypothetically) *would* make under the ideal conditions.

Roderick Firth (1952) has proposed that we consider the judgements which *would* be made by an 'ideal observer', i.e. someone who met, or at least approached, the following ideal conditions:

(i) One knows all the relevant facts.
(ii) One has the ability to imagine what it would be like to be others.
(iii) One is disinterested, impartial.
(iv) One is dispassionate, unaffected by emotions.
(v) One is consistent.

While one of course never completely satisfies all these conditions, the more that one does so in the moral judgements one makes, the more confidently one may regard them as sound 'data' for 'confirming' or 'disconfirming' ethical 'hypotheses'.

There are special problems with conditions (iii) and (iv). Admittedly, they have some plausibility. We normally think that we have to be careful that our moral sense is not distorted by self-interest or blind anger or some such thing. But we might well wonder whether Firth's ideal observer doesn't become so dispassionate, so lacking in emotion, that he just won't care about anything. An anaesthetized observer might make no judgements. On the other hand, to build in specifically *moral* emotions (e.g. desire to do one's duty, a sense of fair play) may be question-begging. It can look as though we would simply be building in an affection for some particular moral value. But we can hardly just assume moral values in employing a 'method' which is supposed to justify moral values.

Perhaps there are ways of overcoming the above problem. In any case, Firth's concern with impartiality is not unlike the next method.

3 THE CONSTRUCTION OF AN IMPARTIAL, OR SOCIAL, POINT OF VIEW

One mark of a moral judgement is that it is not a mere indication of personal self-interest, but is a judgement which tries to take some broader, more impartial standpoint. If we require 'objectivity' in moral judgements, this should not necessarily be taken to mean 'true to the facts', but perhaps something more like 'impartial'. This suggests a rather different sense of the word 'objective' from that defined in (D2) of chapter 8. In the sense of (D2), the opposite of 'objective' is 'subjective', in sense (D1). However, in the present sense, the opposite of 'objective' is something more like 'biased' or 'partial'. There is an important tradition in moral philosophy which regards moral judgements as judgements issued from some impartial, or social, or general point of view, rather than from the point of view of the interests of any one individual or group. Rousseau spoke of the 'general will' (in contrast to all the 'particular wills'). Kant spoke of legislation in a 'realm of ends'. Hume (1739), on occasion, spoke of the necessity of choosing 'some common point of view' in trying to discuss moral questions. Bentham tended to regard moral judgements on an analogy to individuals' judgements of self-interest, except in the crucial respect that they make an appeal to the 'interest of the community' rather than to any particular individual's interest. Sidgwick (1874) spoke of taking 'the point of view of the universe' in making moral judgements. Even Firth (1952), in so far as he includes conditions like (iii) and (iv), may be seen as a part of this tradition.

But a real difficulty is whether talk about such a 'point of view' makes any sense, or, alternatively, whether the notion of 'impartiality' can be explained further. Perhaps what we find in both Nietzsche and Marx, two debunkers of morality, is an attack on just this notion of 'impartiality'. Perhaps the suggestion, for different reasons in the two cases, is that the claim to impartiality implicit in moral judgements is always a sham. However, a recent attempt to make the notion of impartiality clear and explicit can be found in John Rawls' *A Theory of Justice* (1971: ch. 3). The rough idea is that a set of duty-imposing rules for solving conflicts which can arise between individuals may be seen as *impartial* provided it meets the following condition: the set of rules would be chosen by a thoroughly self-interested and rational chooser who, while generally informed, was nevertheless kept suitably ignorant of the particular facts which he could use to tailor the rules to his own special advantage (e.g. he would be ignorant of his social position, his race, his talents, his interests). In slightly more detail Rawls' view (somewhat overstated) is as follows:

The Humean model: 'the circumstances of justice'

Rawls subscribes to a certain kind of picture of the human situation. His picture of the human situation belongs to a type which has been very influential in the history of moral philosophy. For example, we find versions of it in the views of Protagoras, Hobbes, Hume, Hart, Mackie, and many others. (That is not to say that the view is totally uncontroversial.) This picture is not itself a moral or normative claim. Rather, it consists of descriptive claims about the human condition, which on this approach is thought to set the problem to which morality might claim to be the solution. It is sometimes called the 'Humean model' of the circumstances of human nature, after David Hume, whose account in *Treatise*, III, ii, 2 was extremely influential. According to the Humean model, the human condition is one of (a) *moderate scarcity* (and easy transfer) of objects of desire, combined with (b) *limited altruism* (or moderate selfishness). The first means there can never be so much of economic and other desired goods that each can have as much as he might want. The second means, not that psychological egoism is true, but only that there is not enough general altruism about to avoid conflicts arising from the fact of moderate scarcity. A third feature is (c) *mutual knowledge*. This means that generally everyone knows that (a) and (b) hold true, and everyone knows that everyone knows, and everyone knows that everyone knows that everyone knows, etc. Usually a fourth feature, more like Hobbes' view than Hume's, is added as well: (d) *vulnerability*: in the absence of social rules and institutions no individual can be secure from attack. Given the scarcity and easy transfer of desired goods and the limited altruism of human beings, no one can be secure from attack from others who also desire the same objects for themselves (or for their families or groups). Features (a) through (d) make the human situation a 'competitive' one, not in all respects, but still in some important and basic respects. This gives rise to what we might call the problem of conflict. Many philosophers in this tradition (see Mackie 1977: ch. 5) analyse the human situation in terms of the 'prisoners' dilemma' which is well known and discussed in game theory.

The above Humean picture is perhaps still too simple in a couple of respects and needs to be modified accordingly. First, conflict arises, not only in regard to basic (economic) goods but also in regard to socially determined goods such as status. Furthermore, conflict also results from 'different individuals' (and groups') different and conflicting conceptions of the good' (Lukes 1985: 32). For example, one's interests are affected by what others admire and praise, as well as by what they revile and blame. Individuals and societies conflict not only about economic goods but also about values and ideals and over conceptions of what is admirable. However, in so far as this is the case, it makes the grounds for conflict even deeper than Hume supposed.

Second, a great many conflicts arise from individuals' (and groups') desires and interests which are to some extent culturally based, e.g. the desire for status, and money. These may differ from society to society. It might look as though this counts against the Humean picture. However, the Humean claim can be modified. It needn't be the claim that all the same conflicts will occur in all societies. It needn't even be the claim that there are some forms of conflict that cannot be eliminated in any possible form of organization. It only need be the claim that no form of social arrangement can overcome *all* forms of conflict simultaneously. To do so requires a degree of altruism and abundance which is just unrealizable. It's like a warped carpet where one can smooth down any one bump only to find other bumps popping up elsewhere.

Some philosophers in the Humean tradition add a fifth feature: (e) *the lack of perfect information and understanding* (Lukes 1985: 33). Even a society of perfect altruists would need to be able to coordinate information about the choices of others. It would seem to require mechanisms for coordinating individual choices. Feature (e) exacerbates the problem of conflict arising from (a) through (d) and creates a problem of coordination even in areas of cooperation, where there are no conflicts. The circumstances of human nature then present us not only with problems of conflict but also with problems of coordination.

The next step for those in the Humean tradition, beyond this characterization of the human situation, is a certain conception of morality (or at least of justice). Philosophers in this tradition think of morality (or justice) as primarily a device for solving these problems of conflict and coordination which arise from the human situation. The question which confronts us, when thinking morally, is to come up with a set of duty-imposing rules which distributes goods and makes for cooperation, where the total set

171

can be seen to be suitably 'impartial' by any rational person considering the matter.

One can get a better grasp of this Humean conception of morality (or justice) by considering what it would be like to reject it. One way to reject it is to find a reason to reject the description of the human situation behind it. Another, related way, would be to reject the possibility of any 'impartial' solution to the problems of conflict in the human situation. This might be the basis of some Marxists' objections to talk of justice, rights, and such. This makes for a very radical interpretation of Marx's rejection of morality talk. On this interpretation Marx's rejection rests on a total rejection of the Humean model of human nature. As such the Marxist objection would not really depend, as it is usually presented, on the genetic claim that all moral beliefs are to be explained in terms of the way they serve the interests of the ruling class. Instead, this radical objection would rest on the very rejection of the Humean model and the conception of morality (justice) that goes with it (see Lukes 1985: ch. 3). This Marxist view is both more optimistic and more pessimistic about human nature than the Humean model. It is much more optimistic about the communist future where, supposedly, the new motivations resulting from that mode of production will overcome all real problems of scarcity, or where altered desires will overcome the problems of conflict and coordination. It is more pessimistic in regard to the present pre-communist mode of production, holding that here the conflicts are even deeper than the Humean picture paints them. Specifically, class conflicts are so deep that talk of impartiality or justice must always be an illusion (see Miller 1984). In the present, justice is an illusory notion. In the future, it will be unnecessary.

Clearly the difference between those who accept the basic Humean approach to morality (or justice, at least) and those who reject it is one of the radical divides in moral and political philosophy. To some extent the difference is a factual one about human nature. Rawls' acceptance of the Humean account of the circumstances of justice is, while not trivial or completely without controversy, still highly plausible. Of course it is at the same time not what is original in Rawls' view, for he shares his basic Humean account of the human situation and the problems it poses with a major stream in moral thinking.

Choice from behind the 'veil of ignorance'

What is somewhat more original in Rawls is the suggestion that an *impartial* set of rules for solving these problems is one which *would* be chosen by a (quite imaginary) rational chooser who was given the choice of what set of rules would govern the society he was in, where:

(i) The chooser is completely self-interested (i.e. out to maximize his own non-moral good). In particular, we are to imagine him as having no moral or ideological interests (unlike Firth's ideal observer).

(ii) The chooser is rational, e.g. he makes no logical mistakes.

(iii) The chooser has all the *knowledge* he may require (compatible with condition (iv) below) concerning *general* facts about society (e.g. facts about inflation or the incidence of crimes).

(iv) The 'veil of ignorance' condition: The chooser is kept suitably *ignorant* of all the respects in which he is different from others, including (a) his role, position, status in society, (b) his natural talents, assets, abilities, (c) his likes, dislikes, pursuits, and even (d) the generation to which he belongs.

Rawls argues, first, that the choice problem presented to this (quite hypothetical) chooser behind the 'veil of ignorance' has a rational solution, and one which requires no question-begging moral premises for its solution. (This is a matter for decision theory.) Second, he appears to be arguing that the rules for solving problems of scarcity and conflict which would be thus chosen may be regarded as the most impartial ones. They are impartial, not because the hypothetical chooser was impartial (he was not, he was completely self-interested!), but because the hypothetical choice is made in the face of ignorance of every feature which could have been employed to make the choice partial. The rules chosen, not the chooser, have a claim to impartiality.

Of course Rawls' claims on both these counts are controversial. But for the sake of argument let us concede both these claims. We would then wonder what sorts of rules for solving conflicts (or what ethical theory) this method would justify. Rawls in fact has a great deal to say about that which I can hardly go into here. Again, one might concede all the above to Rawls but still object that this method works only for a certain subclass of moral judgements, i.e. judgements of justice and injustice. However, I tend to think that if Rawls' method is appropriate even for this slightly more limited class of moral judgements it makes a substantial contribution. Finally, it should be noted that even Rawls thinks the results of this veil of ignorance (or impartiality) method have to be weighed against 'data' considerations such as methods (1) or (2) might produce.

Why should I be moral?

Let us suppose Rawls has suitable replies to all the above objections. There is a final objection. This might be an objection to any method, but particularly to any method of sort (3), which tries to construct an impartial, social, or neutral point of view. The possibility of some such rational method for solving conflicts might only provoke the response, 'But why, then, should I be moral? Even if there is an impartial point of view, why should I ever be impartial or look at things from any point of view other than the point of view of *my own* interests?'

However, the question 'Why should I be moral?' is ambiguous. It could either be a request for a rational justification (reasons), or simply a request for motivation. Of course people sometimes know their duty but lack sufficient motivation. Some are weakwilled. A few are sociopaths. Is the request, then, just for a motivational spur (a bribe, a beating, a carrot, a stick, a sermon)? In that case what is appropriate very much depends on the circumstances: encouragement, sympathy, exhortation, conditioning, moral education, a role-model, therapy, threats, punishment. Clearly, how to get people, or oneself, to be moral is not the same issue as what is one's moral duty.

But suppose the request is not for motivation but for a (justifying) reason, i.e. 'Why *should* I be moral?' But then *what sort* of reason is being requested? If it is a *moral* reason, the question seems a bit pointless. Of course one *morally* ought to be moral. Apparently the questioner is requiring some sort of *non-moral* reason or justification for being moral: 'Why (non-morally) should I be moral?' But then this is a very peculiar question for anyone to address *to us* (or to others). Certainly it cannot be a *complaint* or a *claim of right* (e.g. 'What moral right have you to morally condemn me for pursuing my self interest?'), for that is to speak the language of morality, or at least to appeal to some impartial basis in one's dealing with others. A response (in kind) to the question 'Why (non-morally) should I be moral?' might be 'Why are you bothering *us* with all this? Why suppose that we *ought* (morally!) to have any regard for the way you answer your question, or allow it to make the least difference to the way we're going to deal with you?' Thus a person who has rejected all forms of moral discourse cannot easily raise this question in a social context.

Perhaps, then, this is a question one raises to *oneself*, 'in a cool hour' as Butler put it. Some philosophers, such as Plato in the *Republic* (and also Aristotle, I would argue), have taken this question quite seriously and have tried to argue that being a moral (or a 'just') person is a core element in the non-morally good life for human (or social) beings. Other philosophers have thought the question senseless, or question-begging. Its very asking seems to assume that non-moral reasons have priority over moral reasons. Again, the very asking of the question has been alleged to be already the mark of an immoral person, so that the question is not really being asked from some 'neutral' point of view, as it might at first appear. The very asking of the question rules out the possibility of being moral.

All this brings us back to one of the problems originally discussed in chapter 1, the conflict between duty and interest. In the course of these chapters we might seem to have replaced one sort of question – 'What is my moral duty?' – with a different question – 'Why (non-morally) should I do what is (admittedly) my moral duty?' This is some sort of progress. At least the critic of morality is no longer going about putting it that morality is somehow 'subjective', or 'personal', or 'existential', or 'situational', or 'solipsistic', or 'relative', or exquisitely hopeless in some other way. He now concedes that there might be some rational, 'objective' (in the sense of impartial) basis for some of our judgements of moral right and wrong. But now he says (although not to us but only to himself), 'So even if there is a moral right and wrong, why should I do it?' To others, such a person now seems very much less like the sage or the guru, and rather more like the social parasite. And even he might begin to wonder whether he wants to be that sort of person.

FURTHER READING

Sidgwick (1874) gives a classical exposition of the 'data' method, as, from a different direction, do Prichard (1949), Broad (1949–50), and Ross (1930). Hume (1777) employs something like the 'data' method to discuss what qualities the moral sentiment is directed toward. Brandt (1959: ch. 10) and Firth (1952) employ the 'qualified attitude method'.

Rawls (1971) and Richards (1971) utilize the constructivist method. Gauthier (1986) and Grice (1967) give contractualist accounts. Hart (1961), Mackie (1977), and Lukes (1985) explore the constraints imposed on morality by the 'Humean' conditions of justice. Historical sources are Hobbes (1651: Pt I, esp. chs 6, 10, 11, 13, 14, 15) and Hume (1739). Miller (1984) criticizes the constructivist idea of 'impartiality' as ideological, while Williams (1985) offers somewhat different objections. Snare (1975a) discusses Rawls' constructivism.

There are many good discussions of the 'prisoners' dilemma'. Basic accounts are Luce and Raiffa (1957), Jeffrey (1965: 11–12), and Schelling (1960). More recent discussions include Brams (1975), Gauthier (1967), and Pettit (1986). Mackie (1977) gives a simple exposition, while Parfit (1979; 1986: chs 2, 3, 4) is difficult.

Plato, in the *Republic* (esp. the discussion by Glaucon and Adeimantus in Bk II), and Scriven (1966) seek to convince the amoralist that moral commitment is in his self-interest. Bradley (1927) gives a classic but unclear discussion. Hospers (1961: ch. 11) answers in effect 'Because it is right'. Prichard (1912) argues that the question involves a mistake. Snare (1980) and Williams (1985) argue that the question has a practical answer in the moral commitment of the community.

Bibliography

Adkins, A. (1960) *Merit and Responsibility*, Oxford: Oxford University Press.

Alston, W. (1967) 'Pleasure', in P. Edwards (ed.), *The Encyclopedia of Philosophy*, vol. 6, New York: Macmillan.

—— (1968) 'Moral attitudes and moral judgements', *Nous* 2, 1–23.

Aquinas, *Summa Theologica*.

Anscombe, G. (1958) 'Modern moral philosophy', *Philosophy* 33, 1–19.

—— (1967) 'On the grammar of "Enjoy"', *Journal of Philosophy* 64, 607–14.

Aristotle, *Nicomachean Ethics*, Bk V, 11–14; Bk X, 1–5.

Aronfreed, J. (1968) *Conduct and Conscience: The Socialization of Internalized Control Behaviour*, New York: Academic Press.

Ayer, A.J. (1936) *Language, Truth and Logic*, London: Victor Gollancz.

—— (1959) 'On the analysis of moral judgements', *Philosophical Essays*, London: Macmillan.

Baier, K. (1958) *The Moral Point of View*, Ithaca, NY: Cornell University Press.

Barnes, B. and Bloom, D. (1982) 'Relativism, rationalism, and the sociology of knowledge', in M. Hollis and S. Lukes (eds), *Rationality and Relativism*, Oxford: Blackwell.

Bayles, M. (ed.) (1968) *Contemporary Utilitarianism*, New York: Anchor.

Benedict, R. (1932) *Patterns of Culture*, Harmondsworth: Penguin.

Bennett, J. (1966) 'Whatever the consequences', *Analysis* 26, 83–102.

Bentham, J. (1780) *An Introduction to the Principles of Morals and Legislation*.

Black, M. (1966) 'The gap between "is" and "should"', *Philosophy* 41, 165–81.

Bradley, F.H. (1927) *Ethical Studies*, 2nd edn, Oxford: Oxford University Press.

Brams, S.J. (1975), 'Newcomb's problem and the prisoner's dilemma', *Journal of Conflict Resolution* 19, 596–612.

Brandt, R. (1959) *Ethical Theory*, Englewood Cliffs, NJ: Prentice-Hall.

—— (1976) 'The psychology of benevolence and its implications for philosophy', *Journal of Philosophy* 73, 429–53.

—— (1979) *A Theory of the Good and the Right*, Oxford: Clarendon Press.

Broad, C.D. (1930) *Five Types of Ethical Theory*, London: Routledge & Kegan Paul.

—— (1949–50) 'Egoism as a theory of motives', *Hibbert Journal* 48; reprinted in C.D. Broad (1952) *Ethics and the History of Philosophy*, London: Routledge & Kegan Paul.

—— (1952) *Ethics and the History of Philosophy*, London: Routledge & Kegan Paul.

Buchanan, A.E. (1983) *Marx and Justice*, London: Methuen.

Burnyeat, M. (1976) 'Protagoras and self-refutation in Plato's *Theaetetus*', *Philosophical Review* 85, 172–95.

Butler, J. (1726) *Fifteen Sermons Preached at the Rolls Chapel*.

Campbell, K. (1981) 'Naturalism in moral philosophy', *Proceedings of the Russellian Society* 6, 12–22.

Chalmers, A. (1976) *What is This Thing Called Science?* St Lucia, Queensland: University of Queensland Press.

Churchland, P. (1984) *Matter and Consciousness*, Cambridge, Mass.: MIT Press.

Clarke, S. (1706) *Discourse upon Natural Religion*.

Cohen, G.A. (1978) *Karl Marx's Theory of History: A Defence*, Oxford: Clarendon Press.

Cohen, S. Marc (1971) 'Socrates on the definition of piety', *Journal of the History of Philosophy* 11, 1–13.

Cooper, N. (1981) *The Diversity of Moral Thinking*, Oxford: Clarendon Press.

Copleston, F. (1963) *A History of Philosophy*, New York: Doubleday.

Cudworth, R. (1731) *A Treatise Concerning Eternal and Immutable Morality*.

Davidson, D. (1973–4) 'On the very idea of a conceptual scheme', *Proceedings and Addresses of the American Philosophical Association* 47, 5–20.

Duncan-Jones, A. (1962) *Butler's Moral Philosophy*, Harmondsworth: Penguin.

Duncker, K. (1939) 'Ethical relativity?' *Mind* 48, 39–57.

Edel, A. and Edel, M. (1959) *Anthropology and Ethics*, Springfield, Ill.: Thomas.

Edwards, P. (ed.) (1967) *The Encyclopedia of Philosophy*, New York: Macmillan.

Elster, J. (1982) 'Sour grapes', in A.K. Sen and B. Williams (eds) *Utilitarianism and Beyond*, Cambridge: Cambridge University Press.

—— (1986) *An Introduction to Karl Marx*, Cambridge: Cambridge University Press.

Feinberg, J. (1975) *Reason and Responsibility*, Belmont, Cal.: Wadsworth.

Festinger, L. (1957) *A Theory of Cognitive Dissonance*, Stanford: Stanford University Press.

Feyerabend, P. (1975) *Against Method*, London: New Left Books.

Field G.C. (1921) *Moral Theory*, New York: E.P. Dutton.

Finnis, J. (1983) *Fundamentals of Ethics*, Oxford: Clarendon Press.

Firth, R. (1952) 'Ethical absolutism and the ideal observer', *Philosophy and Phenomenological Research* 12, 317–45.

Fishkin, J.S. (1980) 'Relativism, liberalism and moral development', in R. Wilson and G.J. Schochel (eds) *Moral Development and Politics*, New York: Wiley.

—— (1984) *Beyond Subjective Morality*, New Haven, Conn.: Yale University Press.

Fletcher, J.F. (1966) *Situation Ethics: The New Morality*, Philadelphia, Pa: Westminster Press.

Flew, A. (ed.) (1983) *A Dictionary of Philosophy*, rev. edn, London: Macmillan.

Foot, P. (1958) 'Moral arguments', *Mind* 67, 502–13.

Frankena, W. (1930) 'The naturalistic fallacy', *Mind* 48, 464–77; reprinted in W. Sellars and J. Hospers (eds) (1952) *Readings in Ethical Theory*, New York: Appleton-Century-Crofts.

—— (1958) 'Obligation and motivation in recent philosophy', in A.I. Melden (ed.) *Moral Philosophy*, Seattle: University of Washington Press.

—— (1970) *Moral Concepts*, Oxford: Oxford University Press.

—— (1973) *Ethics*, 2nd edn, Englewood Cliffs, NJ: Prentice-Hall.

Freud, S. (1913) *Totem and Taboo*, Vienna: Hugo Hiller.

—— (1930) *Civilization and Its Discontents*, London: Hogarth Press.

Gauthier, D. (1967) 'Morality and advantage', *Philosophical Review* 76, 460–75.

—— (1986) *Morals by Agreement*, Oxford: Oxford University Press.

Gay, J. (1731) *Fundamental Principles of Virtue or Morality*.

Geach, P. (1972) 'Plato's *Euthyphro*', in *Logic Matters*, Oxford: Blackwell.

Gosling, J. (1969) *Pleasure and Desire*, Oxford: Clarendon Press.

Grice, G.R. (1967) *The Grounds of Moral Judgement*, Cambridge: Cambridge University Press.

Griffin, J. (1986) *Well-being: Its Meaning, Measurement and Moral Importance*, Oxford: Clarendon Press.

Guthrie, W.K.C. (1962) *A History of Greek Philosophy*, Cambridge: Cambridge University Press.

Hancock, R. (1960) 'The refutations of naturalism in Moore and Hare', *Journal of Philosophy* 57, 326–34.

—— (1974) *Twentieth Century Ethics*, New York: Columbia University Press.

Hare, R.M. (1952) *The Language of Morals*, Oxford: Clarendon Press.

—— (1954–5) 'Universalizability', *Proceedings of the Aristotelian Society* 55.

—— (1963) *Freedom and Reason*, Oxford: Clarendon Press.

Harman, G. (1977) *The Nature of Morality*, New York: Oxford University Press.

Harrison, G. (1979) 'Relativism and tolerance', in P. Laslett and J. Fishkin (eds) *Philosophy, Politics and Society*, 5th series, Oxford: Blackwell.

Hart, H.L.A. (1961) *The Concept of Law*, Oxford: Oxford University Press.

Helm, P. (1981) *Divine Commands and Morality*, Oxford: Oxford University Press.

Herskovits, M. (1947) *Man and His Works*, New York: Alfred Knopf.

Hesse, M. (1980) *Revolutions and Reconstructions in the Philosophy of Science*, Hassocks: Harvester.

Hobbes, T. (1651) *Leviathan*.

Hollis, M. and Lukes, S. (eds) (1982) *Rationality and Relativism*, Oxford: Blackwell.

Hospers, J. (1961) *Human Conduct*, New York: Rupert Hart-Davis.

Hudson, W.D. (ed.) (1970) *Modern Moral Philosophy*, London: Macmillan.

Humberstone, L. (1979) Ethics lecture notes, Monash University (unpublished).

Hume, D. (1739) *Treatise of Human Nature*.

—— (1777) *Enquiry Concerning the Principles of Morals*.

Jeffrey, R.C. (1965) *The Logic of Decision*, New York: McGraw-Hill.

Kant, I. (1785) *Foundations of the Metaphysics of Morals*.

Kaufmann, W. (1968) *Nietzsche: Philosopher, Psychologist, Antichrist*, New York: Princeton University Press.

Kerner, G.C. (1966) *The Revolution in Ethical Theory*, Oxford: Clarendon Press.

Kierkegaard, S. (1941) *Concluding Unscientific Postscript*, trans. D.F. Swanson, Princeton, NJ: Princeton University Press.

Kohlberg, L. (1969) 'Stage and sequence', in D.A. Goslen (ed.) *Handbook of Socialization Research*, Chicago: Chicago University Press.

Kuhn, T. (1970) *The Structure of Scientific Revolutions*, 2nd edn, Chicago: Chicago University Press.

Ladd, J. (ed.) (1973) *Ethical Relativism*.

Locke, D. (1968) 'The trivializability of universalizability', *Philosophical Review* 78, 25–44.

Louden, R. (1984) 'On some vices of virtue ethics', *American Philosophical Quarterly* 21, 227–36.

Luce, R.D. and Raiffa, H. (1957) *Games and Decisions*, New York: Wiley.

Lukes, S. (1985) *Marxism and Morality*, Oxford: Clarendon Press.

McDowell, J. (1973) *Theaetetus: Translated with Notes*, Oxford: Clarendon Press.

MacIntyre, A. (1957) 'What morality is not', *Philosophy* 32, 325–38.

—— (1966) *A Short History of Ethics*, New York: Macmillan.

Mackie, J. (1977) *Ethics: Inventing Right and Wrong*, Harmondsworth: Penguin.

Marx, K. (1843) *On the Jewish Question*.

—— (1859) *A Critique of Political Economy*.

—— (1891) *A Critique of the Gotha Programme*.

Medlin, B. (1957) 'Ultimate principles and ethical egoism', *Australasian Journal of Philosophy* 35, 111–18.

Meiland, J.W. and Krausz, M. (eds) (1982) *Relativism: Cognitive and Moral*, Notre Dame, Ind.: University of Notre Dame Press.

Mill, J.S. (1859) *On Liberty*.

—— (1861) *Utilitarianism*.

Miller, R. (1984) *Analysing Marx*, Princeton, NJ: Princeton University Press.

Monro, D.H. (1967) *Empiricism and Ethics*, Cambridge: Cambridge University Press.

Moore, G. (1903) *Principia Ethica*, Cambridge: Cambridge University Press.

—— (1912) *Ethics*, Oxford: Oxford University Press.

—— (1959) 'A defence of common sense', in *Philosophical Papers*, London: Macmillan.

More, H. (1668) *Encheiridion Ethicum*.

Nagel, T. (1970) *The Possibility of Altruism*, Oxford: Clarendon Press.

Narveson, J. (1967) *Morality and Utility*, Baltimore, MA: Johns Hopkins University Press.

Nielsen, K. (1966) 'Ethical relativism and the facts of cultural relativity', *Social Research* 33, 531–51.

Nietzsche, F. (1967) *On the Genealogy of Morals*, trans. W. Kaufmann and R.J. Hollingdale, New York: Vintage.

Nowell-Smith, P.H. (1954) *Ethics*, Harmondsworth: Penguin.

Paley, W. (1785) *The Principles of Moral and Political Philosophy*.

Parfit, D. (1979) 'Prudence, morality and the prisoner's dilemma', *Proceedings of the British Academy* 65, 539–64.

—— (1986) *Reasons and Persons*, Oxford: Oxford University Press.

Pashman, J. (1970) 'Is the genetic fallacy a fallacy?' *Southern Journal of Philosophy*, 57–62.

Pears, D.F. (1984) *Motivated Irrationality*, Oxford: Clarendon Press.

Penelhum, T. (1957) 'The logic of pleasure', *Philosophy and Phenomenological Research* 17, 488–503.

Pepper, S.C. (1958) *The Sources of Value*, Berkeley: University of California Press.

Perry, R.B. (1954) *Realms of Value*, Cambridge, Mass.: Harvard University Press.

Pettit, P. (1986) 'Free-riding and foul dealing', *Journal of Philosophy* 78, 361–79.

Piaget, J. (1948) *The Moral Judgement of the Child*, London: Routledge & Kegan Paul.

Place, U.T. (1956) 'Is consciousness a brain process?' *British Journal of Psychology* 47, 44–50.

Price, R. (1897) 'Review of the principal questions in morals', in L.A. Selby-Bigge (ed.), *British Moralists*, Oxford: Clarendon Press.

Prichard, H. (1912) 'Does moral philosophy rest on a mistake?', reprinted in H. Prichard (1949) *Moral Obligation*, Oxford: Oxford University Press.

—— (1949) *Moral Obligation*, Oxford: Oxford University Press.

Quine, W. (1960) *Word and Object*, New York: Wiley.

—— (1969) *Ontological Relativity and Other Essays*, London: Columbia University Press.

Rachels, J. (1970) 'On moral absolutism', *Australasian Journal of Philosophy* 48.

—— (1986) *The Elements of Moral Philosophy*, New York: Random House.

Rawls, J. (1971) *A Theory of Justice*, Cambridge, Mass.: Harvard University Press.

Regis, E., jr, (1980) 'What is ethical egoism?' *Ethics* 91, 50–62.

Reid, T. (1764) *Essays on the Powers of the Human Mind*.

Richards, D.A.J. (1971) *A Theory of Reasons for Action*, Oxford: Clarendon Press.

Richards, J.R. (1980) *The Sceptical Feminist*, London: Routledge & Kegan Paul.

Robinson, R. (1953) *Plato's Earlier Dialectic*, Oxford: Clarendon Press.

—— (1971) 'Socratic definition', in G. Vlastos (ed.), *The Philosophy of Socrates*, Garden City, NY: Doubleday.

Ross, W. (1930) *The Right and the Good*, Oxford: Clarendon Press.

—— (1939) *Foundations of Ethics*, Oxford: Clarendon Press.

Ryle, G. (1949) *The Concept of Mind*, London: Hutchinson.

—— (1954) 'Pleasure', *Proceedings of the Aristotelian Society*, Supplementary Volume 28, 135–64.

—— (1964) *Dilemmas*, Cambridge: Cambridge University Press.

Sartre, J.-P. (1963) *Existentialism is a Humanism*, trans. P. Mairet, London: Methuen.

Schelling, T.C. (1960) *The Strategy of Conflict*, Oxford: Oxford University Press.

Scott, J.F. (1971) *Internalization of Norms: A Sociological Theory of Moral Commitment*, Englewood Cliffs, NJ: Prentice-Hall.

Scriven, M. (1966) *Primary Philosophy*, New York: McGraw-Hill.

Searle, J. (1964) 'How to derive "ought" from "is"', *Philosophical Review* 73, 43–58.

Selby-Bigge, L.A. (1897) *British Moralists*, 2 vols, Oxford: Clarendon Press.

Sellars, W. and Hospers, J. (eds) (1952) *Readings in Ethical Theory*, New York: Appleton-Century-Crofts.

Sidgwick, H. (1874) *Methods of Ethics*, London: Macmillan.

—— (1886) *Outlines of the History of Ethics*, London: Macmillan.

Skinner, B.F. (1971) *Beyond Freedom and Dignity*, New York: Alfred Knopf.

Slote, M. (1964) 'An empirical basis for psychological egoism', *Journal of Philosophy* 61, 530–7.

Smart, J. (1959) 'Sensations and brain processes', *Philosophical Review* 68, 141–56.

Smart, J. and Williams, B. (1973) *Utilitarianism: For and Against*, Cambridge: Cambridge University Press.

Snare, F. (1975a) 'John Rawls and the methods of ethics', *Philosophy and Phenomenological Research* 36, 100–12.

—— (1975b) 'The argument from motivation', *Mind* 84, 1–9.

—— (1975c) 'The open question as a linguistic test', *Ratio* 17, 122–9.

—— (1977a) 'Dissolving the moral contract', *Philosophy* 52, 301–12.

—— (1977b) 'Three sceptical theses in ethics', *American Philosophical Quarterly* 14, 129–36.

—— (1980) 'The diversity of morals', *Mind* 89, 353–69.

—— (1984) 'The empirical bases of moral scepticism', *American Philosophical Quarterly* 21, 215–26.

Stace, W.T. (1937) *The Concept of Morals*, London: Macmillan.

Stevenson, C.L. (1942) 'Moore's argument against certain forms of ethical naturalism', in P.A. Schlipp (ed.) *The Philosophy of G.E. Moore*, La Salle, Ill.: Open Court, 69–90.

—— (1945) *Ethics and Language*, New Haven, Conn.: Yale University Press.

—— (1967) 'Moore's arguments against certain forms of ethical naturalism', in P. Foot (ed.), *Theories of Ethics*, Oxford: Oxford University Press.

Stove, D. (1978) 'On Hume's is–ought thesis', *Hume Studies* 4, 64–72.

Taylor, P. (1954) 'Four types of ethical relativism', *Philosophical Review* 63, 500–16.

—— (1958) 'Social science and ethical relativism', *Journal of Philosophy* 55, 32–44.

Ten, C.L. (1980) *Mill on Liberty*, Oxford: Clarendon Press.

Urmson, J. (1967) 'Aristotle on pleasure', in J.M.E. Moravscik (ed.) *Aristotle*, New York: Doubleday.

—— (1968) *The Emotive Theory of Ethics*, London: Hutchinson.

—— (1988) *Aristotle's Ethics*, Oxford: Blackwell.

Warnock, G. (1976) *Contemporary Moral Philosophy*, Oxford: Oxford University Press.

Warnock, M. (1960) *Ethics Since 1900*, Oxford: Oxford University Press.

—— (1967) *Existentialist Ethics*, Oxford: Oxford University Press.

Wellman, C. (1963) 'The ethical implications of cultural relativity', *Journal of Philosophy* 60, 169–84.

Westermarck, E. (1932) *Ethical Relativity*, New York: Harcourt Brace.

Whorf, B. (1956) *Language, Thought and Reality*, Cambridge, Mass.: MIT Press.

Wiggins, D. (1976) 'Truth, invention, and the meaning of life', *Proceedings of the British Academy* 62, 331–76.

Williams, B. (1972) *Morality: An Introduction to Ethics*, Cambridge: Cambridge University Press.

—— (1973) 'Egoism and altruism', in *Problems of the Self*, Cambridge: Cambridge University Press.

—— (1974–5) 'The truth in relativism', reprinted in (1981) *Moral Luck*, Cambridge: Cambridge University Press.

—— (1985) *Ethics and the Limits of Philosophy*, London: Fontana.

Wilson, E.O. (1975) *Sociobiology*, Cambridge Ill.: Belknap.

Winch, P. (1958) *The Idea of a Social Science and Its Relation to Philosophy*, London: Routledge & Kegan Paul.

—— (1964) 'Understanding a primitive society', *American Philosophical Quarterly* 1, 307–24.

Wolff, R.P. (1968) *The Poverty of Liberalism*, Boston, Mass.: Beacon.

Index